THE ALASKAN MALAMUTE
NEVER A PRISONER
By Tommy Williams

Photographs: Tommy Williams

Cover Photograph: Noah, in the snow.

To Noah...
You wrote the story,
I merely put it into words.

Contents

Forward

Everyone has a "first." Their first car. Their first love. Hell, some of us even have a first book (of which this is mine). Noah was my first Alaskan Malamute, and part of any first experience is learning. Readers may not agree with the way I handled some aspects of Noah's care (diet, vaccinations, etc.) while others may find it perfectly acceptable. Those with Malamutes, by nature, have strong opinions and certainly I am no exception. However, I do not want the reader to assume the way I did things is the right and only way, but rather just to understand it is the way I did things with Noah. What is written is the way I felt at that time.

There is also quite a bit that wasn't written. One's first book is just like one's first Malamute – It is a learning experience. This story has been justly criticized for opening literally with no orientation. Who am I? What is my age? Where is this taking place? More importantly, how did I arrive at this particular point in my life? Answers to these questions, if provided at all, are vague at best. I understand that this should be as much my story as it is my story with Noah. But my own story isn't all that significant, really. Trust me. The lessons that Noah taught are though. He was truly special. I was just the human lucky enough to get to share my life with him, and I am forever grateful for that opportunity.

I am not a professional writer. There are parts of this book where I just unload information about people, places, or events, and the narrative suffers because of this. I've done my best though to record a dream long after having woken up. Most frustrating of all has been trying to conceptualize complex thoughts and ideas into a limiting written language.

Finally, this book would not have been possible without the help and encouragement of many other people including Leanna Landsmann for her insistence that this story be told, Jim Thomsen for line-editing, Shelly Franz for formatting, Craig Lancaster for additional formatting, and Jessica Park for her invaluable input and advice. Most of all, I am grateful to my wife, Faith, who changed her life to join me on this trail.

Prelude

While difficult for me to remember, there was a time I had not heard of the Alaskan Malamute. Such proud creatures of the Arctic! Completely unaware of this breed's existence, I could still feel an as yet unidentifiable force waiting to manifest itself upon my life. Like the moon's gravitational attraction on the sea, I was keenly aware of a tidal-like exertion pulling at my heart. Years later, I finally recognized the embodiment of that which beckoned me.

Browsing through magazines at a newsstand, I was looking for something to read at work. Club deejays are required to provide little more than a continuous flow of background music, and I would buy anything that might hold my interest for the better part of a five-hour shift.

A quick scan of the military periodicals revealed nothing. Nothing new or interesting in the sports or science-fiction sections either. Over in the pet section, I locked eyes with what appeared to be a wolf, his gaze coming from someplace beyond the pages within. The latest issue of Dog Fancy was dedicated to the Alaskan Malamute, and it was this stunning breed on the cover that caught my attention.

Picking up the magazine off the rack, I quickly thumbed through it. Page after page of these beautiful creatures convinced me to pay the $2.95 "tuition" for an education on my kindred spirit. While rock 'n' roll was playing at work, I read about the Malamute.

Captivated, I was overcome with a strong desire to know more and continued staring at the pictures long after work in my small apartment. Living primarily a solitary existence by choice, I had few interests and even fewer friends. My cats, two Himalayan seal-points, were indifferent to everything but each other. I did enjoy the winter adventure that western New York occasionally provides: ice-skating on frozen ponds and alpine mountaineering in the Adirondacks.

Both activities offered a temporary diversion from my own general dissatisfaction with existence and a brief respite from a nagging question I often puzzled over while laying in bed: "What is the point of it all?" Tonight was different. Drifting off to far away snow-covered lands, I wondered, "What is it like to share life with an Alaskan Malamute?"

A few years later I received an answer. With all the power and fury of an avalanche, Noah descended upon my life. Days fly by like hours now as we run together through an arctic dream.

"The great moments are not those fleeting seconds of glory most people mistake them for, but rather, they are all the days and years of work invested when there is no guarantee of success or that there will ever be a reward."

Shywulfe

Her name is Shy. Short for Shywulfe, the screen name she used when logging on to America Online, I knew her from the gaming chat rooms we both would frequent back when the internet was new for many of us. Connected by telephone modems to service providers, thoughts traveled at a paltry 28,800 bits per second. Even at this slow speed, cyberspace enabled text-based communication in real time with others. Whether it was with a neighbor down the street or a stranger from across the world, our lives were as varied as the places we were from. The Internet allows possibilities.

One night during a lengthy discussion in instant messages, the subject of pets came up. Shy suggested we give our fingers a rest and talk on the phone instead. Screen names often lent themselves to just faceless entities in the virtual world, and it is nice to reaffirm these internet "handles" really do have living breathing humans on the other end.

"Hi, Wild," she said, addressing me by my own screen name.

She had a confident voice, the hypnotic quality of her tone like a drug my ear craved to hear. Picking up the conversation where we had left off less than a minute before online, I asked her again:

"So, do you have any?"

"I've got dogs."

My only pets were the two cats—and a parakeet I had while growing up.

"I always wanted a dog." The envy was unmistakable in my response.

"What breed?"

"Alaskan Malamute."

"Puppy or adult?" she instantly volleyed back.

I had never really thought about this before. There is no arguing puppies are cute, but I would prefer one already grown-up.

"Adult," I responded.

What she said next was something I could never have prepared myself for.

"I breed and show Alaskan Malamutes. Would you like one?"

Unable to engage my mouth to respond, I was having a difficult time wrapping my head around the reality of our conversation. Too often in life, and especially online, people have a tendency to make themselves appear as something more than they truly are. Entire lives have been fabricated with the sole purpose of impressing others. Incredulous, I could only manage to blurt out a single word.

"Really?"

"Yes." The sincerity in her voice reassuring me all

was real. Shy explained: "There's a family that is probably going to return a two-year-old male to me that was from one of my litters. He's a sweet boy, but their newborn has developed allergies that they're blaming on the dog." She emailed pictures of Benson—literally Ben's (BIS BISS Ch. Nanuke's Revolutionary ROM) son. Fingers crossed, I waited patiently for news.

Weeks passed and Benson's owner reluctantly chose to keep him. Shy suggested another one of her dogs and sent me Noah's picture. Thickly coated with black and white fur, his markings were symmetrical. Two white patches sat above his eyes, with a black stripe running down the length of his nose. Sitting in the snow and gazing into the distance, I could not tell what he might have been looking at. The winter fury blowing around him obliterated all other details. I immediately called Shy to let her know I was interested. We made plans to get together the next day. Directions to my heart's desire were e-mailed that evening.

Shy's log cabin was located in western Pennsylvania, about three hours away by car. My racing pulse and butterflies were a consequence of anxiety brought upon by the awkwardness of a first encounter. While I was excited to finally meet her in person, Noah was the purpose of my visit, and I was anxious to see how we would hit it off.

Driving on Interstate 90 was uneventful until I came upon the road construction she warned me of in her email. Traffic was backed up several miles before my exit and moving slowly. How bad could it be? The answer came an hour later and, after leaving pavement, I was now driving on a temporary dirt road. An orange landscape of cones, vests, signs, and flags extended as far as I could see. The acrid smell of tar filled the air, clouds of dust so thick they blocked out the sun.

Turning south on Interstate 79, the scenery abruptly changed. The contrast between busy road construction and quiet rolling acres of cornfield was startling in the afternoon sun.

The log cabin was just as Shy described, situated atop a hill with kennels in the rear. Gravel crunched beneath my tires as I slowly drove up a lengthy driveway and parked in back. A short pathway of patio stones ushered visitors around to the front of the cabin. Knocking on the wooden door triggered a lone, drawn out howl from within. Shy greeted me at the entrance, and I was momentarily stunned by her attractiveness. Bright jade eyes were further enhanced by blonde hair falling past her shoulders. Dressed in a tee shirt and denim, her jeans were faded with both knees ripped out—sexy *and* cool.

"Hi Wild, c'mon in."

Her smile hit me like a punch in the gut. Walking inside, an Alaskan Malamute immediately positioned herself between us and let out a deep-throated "Woo."

Laughing, Shy introduced me to Maija. "She gets jealous."

Looking around, wooden beams and log walls were adorned with many different prints of wolves and Indian maidens. Forest green carpet covered the floors throughout. A curio cabinet held numerous wolf sculptures.

"Are you ready to meet Noah?"

I nodded nervously.

"Wait here. I'll let him and his sister up."

Shy descended a flight of stairs, her appearance into

the basement eliciting a chorus of howls followed by the thundering paws of Noah and another Malamute, Erika, running up to greet me. My God, these dogs are BIG. Soon after this initial shock comes the realization they are also beautiful. Instantly captivated by Noah's warm eyes and soft features, I am in awe of this magnificent creature.

> He stands proud before me, plumed tail held high and waving side to side in a breeze of confidence. Covered in coarse black fur with white undersides, intelligence is reflected within dark brown, almond-shaped eyes. A black bar runs the length of his nose as if smeared with coal, and he wears his mask like a bandit. Powerful shoulders are evident as I wrap my arms around his deep chest. Burying my fingers into the luxurious wooly coat, I can feel a well-muscled body beneath. Like a mass of snow that breaks off and rushes forcefully down a mountainside, Noah was about to storm into my life.

Shy let Noah and Erika out to play in the yard. Sitting together with no distractions allowed us to talk in earnest about the breed for the better part of an hour. I asked if she would like to continue the conversation over a meal. "Yes," was just the answer I was looking for as my stomach was beginning to rumble.

Dinner was at a family-style restaurant, and much of our conversation centered on how I might happily co-exist with a large, active dog in a small apartment. I could easily listen all night about Alaskan Malamutes, but knew Erika was showing the next morning in Canton, Ohio and still needed to be bathed.

"I'd better let you get back to take care of everyone."

"Come to the Canton show with me tomorrow, unless you have other plans? You can spend the night at my place."

Never having seen a dog show before, I eagerly agreed to tag along. Just meeting her a few hours earlier though and having known her only online, I had planned on renting a motel for the evening. But Shy insisted I go back with her. Believing herself a good judge of character, she also correctly reasoned, no one would chance harming her while she was surrounded by eight Alaskan Malamutes and a Siberian Husky.

While Erika was bathed, Noah and I played in the yard. We played hard. Grass-stained and covered with fur, I was filthy from rolling on the ground with my new friend. It was getting late so a shower would need to wait until morning. Noah, Erika, and several other Malamutes were crated for the night. Shy brought out blankets and a pillow, and bid me goodnight.

I bedded down on the floor next to Maija. She seemed friendly enough, and I inched a little closer. Within arm's reach now, I began to scratch her white belly. Resting my head upon her side elicited a low growl. She made her point perfectly clear—a proud Alaskan Malamute will not tolerate being used as a stranger's headrest. Returning to my pillow, I pulled the blanket over my shoulder. Maija continued looking in my direction— not at, but past me, into the darkness. I fell asleep quickly, unaware of the drastic changes about to take place in my life.

Saturday, we were off to the show just as the sun was beginning to rise. Working in a bar, one gets used to staying up late and sleeping in, but I was up that morning when most folks I worked with were just getting home. Shy used a large extended van to get to shows. The back seat had been removed, and five dog crates were neatly arranged, secured to the floor with bungee cords. Packed away in the corner was a grooming table and grooming supplies. Water and treats were within easy reach. Ex-pens* were attached to the front grill of the van. We stopped for gas, and after picking up coffee and ice inside, were on the road with Erika and Noah. Shy was also bringing along a friend's Akita to show.

We pulled into the show grounds at 7 a.m. Several of Shy's friends had arrived earlier, their vans parked, awnings out, and dogs already up on grooming tables. No sooner had I exited the van than Shy brought me over to meet Sandy D'Andrea of Nanuke Kennels, who was busy grooming Noah's sire, Tyler. BIS BISS Am/Can Ch. Nanuke's Take No Prisoners ROM, Tyler is the all-time-winningest Malamute in the history of the breed, with over seventy Best in Shows to his credit. Having produced numerous Best in Show Champions for many years, Sandy is well renowned in the Malamute community. Highly respected as a breeder/owner/handler, she is largely responsible for the high quality and good temperament of Shy's dogs.

A flurry of other introductions ensued before I was put to work assembling ex-pens, filling water buckets, and arranging fans in front of crates. Shy set up a grooming table, and after grooming Noah and Erika, busied herself preparing the Akita to show. This beautiful summer morning had all the makings of a scorcher, and the day was beginning to heat up quickly.

My own work temporarily finished, I wanted to parade around the grounds.

"Is it all right to take Noah for a walk?"

Expecting a nervous look from Shy, she simply reminded me, "Just keep him away from other dogs and watch for overheating."

I slipped a choker over his head and affixed his green lead to it. Noah was happy to leave the ex-pen and explore, stopping every few feet to examine a new smell. All the dogs here were showing, and we walked around the field with purpose, just as if we were entered ourselves. It felt natural having him on the other end of the lead—as if we had always been together.

Returning shortly after the Akitas had finished showing, the Alaskan Malamutes were next. I quickly ushered Noah into his crate. Following behind Shy and Sandy, they led Erika and Tyler to a large tent. Once there, each of them checked in and strapped a number to their arm.

Twelve Alaskan Malamutes, all stacked on a white chalk line, awaited inspection. The judge slowly walked down that line, thoroughly examining every aspect of each dog. It seemed she was spending extra time with Tyler, her hair matching his wolf-gray coat.

Having finished with her individual inspection, she instructed each handler to circle their Malamute once around the fenced ring, and then had them circle together as a group. While the handlers were circumnavigating their Malamutes around the perimeter, she pointed to Tyler, and Sandy ran him to the center of the ring. She then called out a few others, with Best Opposite Sex

(BOS) honors going to Erika.

Stopping at one of the vendors on my walk back to the van, I bought Noah a smoked bone, and he was working on this treat when Shy and Sandy returned with the dogs—and their ribbons. Having won breed, Tyler would be showing again later that afternoon, to represent Alaskan Malamutes in the working group.

Sandy put Tyler back up on the grooming table and worked in conditioner to his coat with a steel comb. Shy was done showing for the day. Leaving the dogs in their shaded crates, we went for lunch, the smell of Italian sausage beckoning from one of the tents. Combined with scents not normally present within a home, food seems more flavorful when eaten outdoors. Wiping sweat from my forehead with a napkin, an iced can of soda is colder under a blistering sun.

We watch as Tyler proves unstoppable, taking the working group and going on to win Best in Show. Packing up afterwards, Shy asks what I thought of it all.

"I had a great time. It's like a carnival minus the rides," I added, "with dogs instead."

Her smile was that of a woman unconvinced. "Well, thanks for coming."

"Seriously, I had a good time, and I learned a lot too."

I had witnessed firsthand one of the *Great Moments*:

Not every dog can be a show dog. Most people aren't interested in showing their dogs; they buy one simply to keep as a pet. The places a dog can be purchased are as varied as the number of breeds. Some people breed dogs as a hobby. Others breed with the intention of generating an income. Neither reason is a good one. The world doesn't need any more puppies from a hobbyist breeder. There are enough dogs already in rescue shelters waiting for homes. Those who breed solely for money (puppy mills fall in this category) are often interested more in the bottom line than what is required to bring a healthy dog into the world. These people are a complete detriment to the dog and its breed.

There are a few who strive to improve the breed. Not as a hobby or way to make extra cash (they know better), but an unconditional love of the dog is driving them. Reputable breeders spend large sums of money on health tests (CHD, CERF, etc) and compare genetics of many different lines, trying to weed out bad temperament, chondrodysplasia, and cataracts. Their goal isn't one of vanity or money, but simply to produce the healthiest and happiest puppies as close to the breed standard as possible. Regardless of how well they succeed in their goal, they accept responsibility of each dog for the entire length of that dog's life.

Conformational showing is an event where a dog's qualities are assessed and impartially judged by others considered experts in that particular breed. What happens when it becomes apparent a dog will not earn a point, let alone the title of champion?

One of Noah's testicles never descended, and Shy made the decision to have her pick of the litter neutered. Unable now to show him, she experienced frustration and possibly a little humiliation. Instead of accepting failure, she continued bringing him to shows with the others. She would bathe and groom him just as though he were entered.

These are the kind of actions that make fanciful dreams we all have a reality few ever realize. The great moments are not those fleeting seconds of glory most people mistake them for, but rather, they are all the days and years of work invested when there is no guarantee of success, or that there will ever be a reward. Often, hard work with no compensation can easily be viewed as wasted time. Labor such as this is not in vain. These are the moments that define a person.

Titles and championships don't really tell me much about Shy's character. What speaks volumes is watching her groom Noah to perfection at a show he wasn't entered in, when it would've been easier to have just left him at home.

We returned to the cabin, and I played in the yard with Noah and Erika while Shy fed the dogs. Knowing she spent every night online, I thought she might enjoy going out for once. Both of us exhausted from the show,

I asked anyway if she was up for a date. Her wide grin indicated a second wind. Showing her as good a time as I had experienced just hours earlier was a tall order to fill, but I was willing to try.

Bar-hopping in town that evening, we eventually came to rest at a small pub called Zipper's. I had been drinking ale and she light liqueurs.

"Time for something different," I exclaimed and instructed the bartender on how to concoct a Brain.

This disgusting mix of peach schnapps, Irish cream, and grenadine, when combined, gives the appearance of a miniature bloody brain floating in the glass. Had I ordered this when we started out, no doubt the evening would have ended early. Several shots later, though, she slammed back the drink with impunity. Shy smiled, "We need to call it a night while I can still walk, I have to bring the dogs in yet."

Arriving back at her place just after midnight, Shy asked me to let each dog out of the kennel to go potty, and then wait for her signal. Yelling every time she was ready, I opened the kennel doors. Each dog had a crate in the basement with a peanut butter biscuit waiting inside. In pairs, the dogs ran through the doorway and down the stairs, Maija being the last one in.

It was dark in the country. Leaning against her van, I watched summer constellations making their rounds, the Milky Way strewn across the sky. Shy met me back outside. Passion arced between our bodies as her lips met mine. Taking my hand, she led the way into her cabin and up to the loft. Filled with nothing but a computer and a daybed, this is where she spent all her nights while online.

The physical attraction between us was strong. She

had consumed a considerable amount of alcohol, though, and I did not want my memories of this place tarnished by any action she might regret later. Knowing destiny allows as many opportunities as necessary for its fulfillment, I drifted off to sleep with her blonde hair in my face.

I did not want to leave this enchanted place fearful it would all end upon waking up. Shy assured me it was no dream. Driving back to Rochester, my thoughts were occupied with Shy, Noah, and an entirely different way of life revolving around Alaskan Malamutes. My banal existence verified upon returning home, I turned on the computer. There was a new e-mail waiting:

> *I just wanted to have this here for you when you got home. I had an absolutely wonderful time this weekend. Your the greatest and soooooooo sweet. Dang, I miss you already! :::grins::: I think Noah does too. He is still crashed out from all the playing. I hope your drive home was good and not too much traffic. I can't wait to see you.*
> *Love,*
> *Shy***

We would be together again in a few days. The plan was for me to meet her at the cabin Thursday, and we would travel back to Rochester the following afternoon.

A few days. It does not sound like much. this same feeling I had as a child on Christmas Eve. I was unable to sleep, and morning seemed like it would never come. Even at 5 a.m., dawn was still an eternity away. Stretch this feeling now over four days, and I begin to understand the length of geological epochs.

In the meantime, we talked. We talked every night, for hours at a time, about everything. Sometimes, we talked so much my ear hurt from holding the phone against it. When we were not talking, we were IMing and e-mailing each other:

> *Sorry about my stupid phone. I guess I'd better invest in a non-cordless one. I really hope I can talk to you again later tonight. I forgot to ask you how your day went? Good I hope. Mine was pretty uneventful - bills and mowing the lawn. Eeeeewwwwww. ::grins::: Oh, and by the way, I bought you a present. :::giggles::: I do miss you hun and I'll talk with you tonight.*
> *Love,*
> *Shy***

My gift, a brass keychain with an etched wolf on one side and a message on the reverse, was a continual reminder of my new relationship. All week long, e-mails continued back and forth.

> *Geez, I hope you don't get tired of my emails. I just wanted to tell you something. I know you say that your heart is in bits and pieces, but I think that you have a big heart that is filled with love, and it shows in your eyes when I look in them. I love to listen to your voice, and I miss it when we hang up*

the phone. You are very straight forward, and I love that too. You have a romantic soft side that makes me melt, a caring loving side that makes me smile, and a tough strong side that makes me feel safe. I love being with you, and I can't wait to see you again. ::::::puts her hand over his mouth so he can't say anything::::::

You, in my eyes, are wonderful. See you soon hun.
Love,
Shy**

Several relationships prior to my one with Shy had not worked out. And having been hurt before, I was reluctant to follow my heart's lead. I had no idea where this wonderful relationship was heading but held on tight, hoping just to enjoy the ride. The next morning I would be on my way back to that magical log cabin.

Familiar with the route now, my drive to Meadville seemed much quicker. There are things too good to be true. How was Shy going to react when we met again? I was uncertain and did not know what to expect. I would be finding out soon enough.

There was the cabin. The dogs were kenneled, with the exception of Noah and Erika playing together in the yard. Waiting there to greet me at the gate, Shy wrapped her arms around me, a full minute passing before she allowed me to breathe again. It really *was* to good, and all of it true as well.

The next afternoon, we headed to my place in Rochester. Following close behind in her van, Shy was bringing along Maija, Taylor, Erika, and of course, Noah.

A friend would be looking after her other dogs for the next few days while she was away.

Just west of Buffalo, we stopped at a rest area where we could let the dogs out to stretch and go potty. Watching the reaction of others, it appears unlikely they have ever seen Alaskan Malamutes before. Some approach to get a better look and ask a question or two, but most just stare in awe at the sight of one sled dog after another leaving the van for a quick romp in the grass.

The sky was beginning to redden upon our arrival in Rochester. Since it was completely impractical (and nearly impossible) to house four Alaskan Malamutes in a small apartment, we left them in the van. The summer heat and vandalism were big concerns. A large fan placed in front of the crates was powered by running an extension cord from my apartment to the parking lot, and the windows were covered with a light-reflective tarp. Having parked in a spot directly across from my bedroom window allowed us to easily monitor whether or not someone was trespassing. The dogs themselves were a deterrent, with one neighbor pointing out, "Nobody wants to go near a van full of large, vicious wolves."

Fully aware of Noah's predatory nature, I knew it would never be wise to leave him unattended with other animals. So I made alternative arrangements for my cats. Still, we were curious how he would react seeing an animal other than a Malamute for the first time. I locked one feline in the bedroom and while cradling the other in my arms, Shy brought Noah in on lead. Face to face with this large, woolly beast in the doorway, I felt his body stiffen. His blue eyes expanded the size of pie plates, and springing away from me with a jump worthy of an

Olympic medal, he was off and running at full throttle. Noah was after him immediately. Shy held on tight to the lead as my cat scurried to safety under a kitchen cabinet. We let Noah wander around and sniff for a few minutes, before bringing him back to the van.

I called my neighbor to come adopt her new cats. Noah was staying.

Shy returned to her cabin the next day. Shortly after her departure, I took Noah out, and while he explored, I tried convincing myself this Alaskan Malamute was real and not some phantom indicative of a mind gone bad. We walked and played together for hours. I called Shy once we were back to let her know all was well.

"How did it go?" She asked.

"We had a great time today and I think I tired him out. He's just sniffing around the living room right now."

Circling around on the carpet then slowly inching his back paws close to his front, Noah squatted down and excreted a big stinky dump. Unbelievable. There had been plenty of time to go while we were out.

Laughter on the other end of the phone ensues and Shy explains, "He's just testing your mettle, Wild."

Shy liked to send reminders she was thinking of me. Sometimes they were cards or letters, but most often there were e-mails letting me know I was loved. Flowers clearly send a message of affection, and one morning Noah and I were confronted at the door by some strange guy thrusting a dozen long-stemmed roses at us.

They were from Shy.

Before high-speed broadband connections, getting online was often an arduous experience that required dialing into one of an Internet Service Provider's telephone modems. During peak times, it could take over an hour to get through and make a connection. So bad were wait times that my ISP was appropriately nicknamed America Offline by its many disgruntled users across the continent.

> *Guess what? I got online. So..... I just wanted to send you a little message before I went to bed. You are so very special to me, and I thank god that you came into my life. I love you so much already, and I feel so close to you, but each day that passes my feelings get even stronger. When we are together I feel so happy, and the rest of the world doesn't even exist. No one ever made me feel that way before. When the day comes that we won't have to say goodbye anymore will be my dream come true. When you go to sleep tonight, smell the roses and dream of me. I will meet there.*
> *All my love,*
> *Shy****

I eagerly anticipated each visit to see Shy, and Noah enjoyed riding along. We were taking this journey often.

> Packing is always done the night before. A rucksack for Noah contains his stainless steel bowl, food for three days, treats, bones, and toys. My bag is stuffed with clothes, casual wear like sweats to sleep and run in and denim and leather in case we go out. My most important attire

consists of army camouflage pants, a cutoff tee shirt, and a pair of boots. It is this "outfit" that allows me to wrestle with eight Alaskan Malamutes and a Siberian Husky without ever looking dirty.

Our morning together has become routine. Noah waits on the bed for me to open my eyes. He is very vocal, and once they're open, there is no closing them. He pounces on me beneath the sheets, relentless in rousing me out of bed. I quickly dress, and together we head to the kitchen. Picking up his food bowl, the "wooing" starts in earnest. Noah's hungry, and the sound of kibble hitting the stainless steel sends him into a frenzy. Water is added to moisten the food and walk the meal over to his crate. Noah is bounding behind me, gobs of saliva flying in all directions. While he downs the kibble, I fill his water bucket. Hearing the metallic sound of the bowl clanking against his crate, I know he's finished. Letting him out, Noah eagerly fits his head into the collar. With the green lead in my hand, we are out the door for a two-mile run.

After a shower, I wash toast down with coffee. I don't mind that it's still early today. The drive to Pennsylvania is long, but always enjoyable. Even if we're on the road by half past ten, the earliest we can hope to arrive is two o'clock in the afternoon. I load up the car with our stuff and then come back to get Noah. He senses something is going to happen, but is unable to put his paw on it. When I bring out the red gas can I use to carry Noah's water in while traveling, he realizes what's up. We've received some pretty strange looks from people when they watch him drink the contents from that can.

The car fueled and washed, metallic blue finish sparkles under the bright sunlight. An '87 IROC Z-28 Camaro with T-tops, it is built for summer. Noah likes rides and travels well. A blue sheet covers the back seat, and this is where he spends most of the trip working on a bone.

Finally, we are on the road. Whatever worries or concerns I may have are left behind. The plan is to put over two hundred miles between them and myself. Not that it matters anyway, with an Alaskan Malamute beside me, everything else in life is secondary.

Driving through the city of Rochester is a necessary evil. We eventually pick up I-90 in Leroy and travel west for the next two hours. Exit 5 in Erie puts us on I-79 south, and from here we are thirty-five minutes away. The rolling hills between Erie and Pittsburgh remind me of how one's life fluctuates. Throughout the ups and downs and before we reach our destination, I am fortunate enough to share this journey with my Northern companion in the back seat.

Why is it anticipation grows as something wonderful approaches? Anticipation must be inversely proportional to time. We exit 36-A. Another turn and we pass a convenience store on the left. Up a hill and pull the wheel right. Keep left at the "Y".

No longer looking at road signs, I am navigating by heart. There it is up on the left. This is one of the few times I see something and am aware of it before Noah is. Pulling up the stone drive, Noah realizes it too—we have arrived.

Pacing back and forth, Erika is the only Malamute out. Noah emerges from the confines of the car and runs toward the kennels. Walking over, I open the gate allowing access to the second yard. Noah marks territory while I open Erika's kennel. Bolting after her brother, they are reunited and will remain inseparable the entire visit. Although Noah is my world, and likewise, I am his, for three days I will not exist. This log cabin in Pennsylvania is a magical place. I walk up the steps and Maija is there to greet me at the door.

With the warm summer finally past, days were growing shorter and nights much cooler. Autumn ushered in the last big event for Malamutes. The Alaskan Malamute Nationals is an all-breed show held yearly, each time in a different location. Shy was taking several of her dogs to Louisville, Kentucky for competition and would be leaving the next morning. Noah would not be going along. I called that evening to wish her luck.

It is Saturday night and all the dogs are getting ready for the Nationals. Shy is busy bathing Erika and Maija. She is taking everyone, and Noah's entire family will be there. He will remain home with me, both of us missing out on the fun and excitement. AKC rules state that a dog needs both testicles for conformational showing. How unfortunate. Everyone's opinion is that he would have done well in conformation showing—including the Nationals. Some feel life isn't fair. They're right—it's not. The sooner one realizes this, the happier one will be.

A beautiful dog born with an undescended testicle, Noah is considered by some to be incomplete. However, testicles don't make a dog any more than they make a man. He is 100% Malamute and more than adequate for me. I'm glad he was neutered, otherwise he would be at Shy's, getting ready for the show with the others. He would not be here with me right now. Not ever. We may miss the show's fun and excitement, but testicles are a small price for us to be together.

Shy finished showing for the year and planned to start working after the holiday season. While living the life of a princess, she realized it would not last indefinitely. The time was fast approaching where she needed to start making an income. We talked about moving in together and began looking at places in New York.

Requirements for safely living and caring for Alaskan Malamutes are many. Our search for a suitable home was unsuccessful. Shy returned to Pennsylvania just before Thanksgiving, and I was driving down a day later for dinner with her family. She took Noah back with her to be bathed, and Taylor remained with me for the night.

Taylor understands her place in the pack and is well-behaved. Unlike Noah, she is a lover and quick to show affection by licking and rubbing her head against me. The most striking difference is evident when she is on lead. Walking with Noah is like having a locomotive pulling on the other end. Taylor is similar to a sports car, her movement fluid and easy to control.

I returned Taylor shortly before dinner. Noah and Erika, having played for hours before resting in the kennel, were uninterested in my arrival until discovering my pocket contained treats. Our own meal was the traditional Thanksgiving spread. Just before pumpkin pie was served, Shy surprised everyone at the table by informing all she was getting a tattoo.

I had been inked a few weeks earlier, claw marks tearing through the skin of my right arm similar to the welts Noah leaves after we play. Shy made an appointment with the same talented woman that rendered mine. Unable to decide between two different wolf designs, she chose both.

Six inches of new snow covered the ground Christmas Day. A decorated pine tree stood in one corner of her cabin, and a stocking for each dog hung on the fireplace mantle. Looking closer, I also spotted one with my name on it. We exchanged gifts, the knitted wolf blanket I received being especially timely.

Hired locally, Shy started working that January, and the overnight shifts made visiting difficult. Having developed many new friendships on the job, she was spending what little free time her schedule allowed socializing with them. We began to drift apart as people do when their lives lead them in different directions. By April, the distance between us was so great we were no longer together.

Shy had married young, and when that fell apart after fourteen years, she took the opportunity to experience things most others do while still in their late teens and early twenties. I always felt that our relationship was transitory, never once though considering how I might be affected when it ended. But who among us ever worries about waking in the middle of a beautiful dream?

Shy touched my heart like no other. Even though she was no longer an intimate part of my life, I look back on the time we spent together with great fondness. Many things never to be shared again, we will always have in common our love for an Alaskan Malamute named Noah.

Our morning started out just like every other—Noah standing over me in bed, drooling on my face. My Alaskan Malamute was hungry, and it was time to eat. Familiar with the routine, he watches me quickly dress, and then walk to the kitchen to fill his stainless steel bowl with kibble.   When he finishes eating, we go outside to discover what the new day has in store for us.

Today was different.   Like opening the oven door to check on something baking, my face was met with a blast of hot air as we walked outside.   I had known this day would eventually come.   Just as Shy was gone now from our lives, the warning signs were there that our world of snow and cold was also coming to an end.   The ice castles had melted a month before. We once could run across a sheet of ice, but now were forced to walk around a pond instead. Rising in the East over the fir trees, Orion used to greet us each evening as we journeyed through the winter landscape. The snow is gone, and he has long since departed as well, having now been replaced by unfamiliar constellations.

Today is a sad day.   I finish brushing out Noah's undercoat.   I mount the air conditioner into the window and pull shut all the drapes.   Our world is getting smaller as winter recedes.   Where once it occupied almost all of North America, it will soon be no larger than this room. Painted white like a glacier with scenes of distant snow-covered places hanging on the walls, it is here we will wait, insulated from the intense summer's heat and burning sun, going outside only to potty or to walk late at night. We will be isolated from other humans.   I miss Shy. However, I find loneliness easier to endure away from other people.

Winter will eventually return again, and Noah will be there with me when it does. I realize now I am better off affixing my hopes on important certainties like that, not on relatively trivial matters as to whether or not someone loves me.

---

*An ex-pen is a fencing system that can be quickly assembled and broken down. It allows dogs a safe area in which to exercise and potty.

"A relationship with an Alaskan Malamute is one that many envy, few can understand, and none can touch."

Nomads of the North

The first few months without Shy were a time of a difficult adjustment. Many of my evenings had been occupied talking with her and gaming together online. Whether she brought her dogs to visit, or I made the trip to Pennsylvania, we spent our weekends together, and it had been my false assumption that we would eventually share more.

No longer able to sleep in the bed we had shared, I now slept on the living room floor next to Noah's crate. Even with the door of his crate left open, he continues sleeping inside. While most humans sleep side by side in physical contact, Noah is content just to bed down with me in close proximity. He provides an enormous amount of emotional support, but the message is clear—he will not be treated as some stuffed animal to be held at night.

I write Shy often, but few letters are sent. Each one seems nothing more than a rehash of the same worn-out topics. A new perspective is needed. What would Noah say if *he* were able to compose a letter to her?

Dear Shy,

I have never before conversed with any word other than "woo," but you probably recognize me. There is much to tell, and I may not get the opportunity to communicate like a human again.

You brought me into this world. You wanted me. My birth was planned with the mating of my father, Tyler, and my mother, Maija. I was no accident. You picked the best possible parents to assure me a healthy body and sound mind. You helped Maija care for me, and my littermates when we were just pups.

I never got to know Wookie or other brothers that well, but did develop a close relationship with my sister, Erika. Sometimes I miss chasing her tail in the yard and wrestling in the kennel. I will always remember the sound of her voice and waking up in the morning with her beside me.

The first year of my life was wonderful. You cared for me. You fed me and bathed me. You gave me a yard to play in and a dry place to sleep. You showed it was alright for others to touch and handle me, and I am therefore not afraid of strangers or children.

You gave much of your time and money because you cared. You sacrificed many things including all of your freedom, friendships, and relationships. You put my needs before your own. You loved me, and by your example you taught me how to love as well.

Love forced you to find me another home. I was happy with you and the others, but you wanted more for me. You wanted someone who could devote their self completely to me, just as I devote myself completely to them—someone that loves me as much as you.

Wild is a good choice. I know he loves me, and you can see it too. I return his love and bring him joy. I don't allow him to wake up lonely. I am there when he opens his eyes, kissing his face. I make sure he exercises each day. I am there when he needs me, whether he knows it or not, sharing both his laughter and tears. I am unsure where your relationship stands with him, but there is no need to worry. I am watching over him.

Thank you for all you did. You provided me with a wonderful past and the promise of happy future. I have many beautiful memories of my first year with you, Shy. Yours was the first face I saw when I entered this world and one I will never forget.

Love,
Noah

Things were not getting any easier as summer arrived. Unable to fill the void left in the wake of her departure, I was mindlessly making my way through each day. Getting by in the absence of someone is not the same as continuing on without that person. Searching for comfort in the familiar, I struggled to find anything remotely similar to what I had known. The futility of my search quickly became obvious, and rightfully so. Relationships are unique to the individuals involved, carved out by experiences shared together.

Not much of a social person to begin with, my contact with others dwindled to almost nothing. Aside from the limited conversation required of me at work or an exchange of pleasantries with the cashier ringing up my groceries, my life was absent of human contact. Interestingly, with no human even remotely an active part of my life, I was no longer lonely. While I had been waiting for a relationship to walk through the front door on two legs, one had run up behind me on all fours and bowled me over. It was not a human that provided the companionship I desperately craved, but an Alaskan Malamute.

My relationship with Noah had grown to a point where it eclipsed everything else. Our world literally resembled a glass snow globe. We two nomads of the North shared our lives together in a winter wonderland others could see, but were unable to enter, as if prevented by the edge of a crystal sphere.

It is not marked on any calendar,
this special day
that had been approaching.

All the signs were here.
The mercury falling
and days growing shorter.
It had been a long time coming
before our world of snow and ice returned.

In anticipation
we have waited for this moment,
like two young lovers
whose wedding day has finally arrived.
It snowed today.
While others run inside
and flee to someplace warm,
we find sanctuary in the cold.
The storehouses of snow have been opened and
Boreal screams his message from the north.
Orion rises opposite the setting sun
        and under the stars we run.
There comes a moment in each of our lives
we wish to halt time
and live those few seconds forever.
Noah and myself concur,
that moment is now.

If you've never lived with an
        Alaskan Malamute—
If you've never shared your life
with a creature of the arctic,
then what I write will be difficult
        to understand at best.
Those that live for the days when
winter snows cover the landscape
and long for Boreal's icy touch

need no explanation.

I am not incapable of loving others
and sympathize for those with
*   whom I am close.*
They may not always be able to recognize
*   my love.*
In a land of ice and snow, wind and cold,
I have bonded with my northern brother.
A relationship with an Alaskan Malamute is
one that many envy, few can understand,
and none can touch.

Alaskan Malamutes participate in dog shows held weekly all across the country. Everything culminates during November at the Nationals, a yearly specialty show held in various locations. This year, Carlisle, Pennsylvania was playing host to the event. Owners, breeders, handlers, and their Malamutes would congregate from all over North America. Wookie, who was currently tearing up the west coast, would be flying in with Mare. Sandy was bringing several of Noah's kin—including his legendary sire, Tyler. Shy entered Erika. Coming along as well with her would be Taylor and Maija.

I did not want Noah missing out on the Nationals for a second time and decided that we too were going to be there. Being altered, he was not eligible for conformational showing events, but could still compete in any of the working competitions. I thought we would try the weight pull and ordered a fancy red harness from Black Ice supplies. Noah began training each evening, with his workout consisting of pulling a tire. He took to this new challenge immediately, and I quickly increased both the weight and distance he was pulling.

Weight-pull harnesses (sometimes called freight harnesses) are slightly different than the X-back harnesses used for dog sledding. A heavily padded, broad chest band spreads the load, and the tug line attaches behind the dog close to the ground instead of on the back just before the tailbone.

Both of us being novices, I was fairly certain we would not bring home any ribbons or hardware from this trip. Still, I wanted something tangible to present him with for all of his hard work. I had a marble and brass trophy created before we left and packed it along with my clothes.

Our arrival in Carlisle was later than I would have liked. The motel parking lots were full of vans here for the Nationals; their license plates from all over the United States and Canada. Accommodations were situated on several acres that also would host numerous agility and pulling events. The motel also contained an indoor events center where conformational showing would take place.

Many of the handlers were out exercising their dogs. Noah visited regularly with other canines during our walks. Each visit, the sight of another dog causes Noah great excitement. His mind races, "Who is this?"... "I know her!"... "What does she smell like today?"... "Let's play!"... "Does your friend have treats?"... "Hey... Let me go potty!"... "Does your pee smell like mine?"... "I think I have to go again—right where you just did."... "I think your friend DOES have treats, and I'll just go and see for myself!"... "Why is HE calling me again?!"... "Let's just run and I'll check your friend for treats later!"

I checked into our room and put Noah on a lead. Mr. Sociable was glad to be outside. It wasn't one or two dogs he saw here. It wasn't ten or twenty either. There were hundreds of Malamutes. I thought his canine brain might short-circuit.

We walked the grounds. Shy and Sandy were parked next to each other. Grooming tables set up, they both were busy prepping dogs for an early morning show. Several young bitches from one of Sandy's recent litters waited patiently in X-pens for their turn. Mare came running up to greet us, eager to meet Noah. I was anxious to see Wookie as well and followed her back to the spot she had staked out.

Jet lag had caught up to him, and he was sleeping in his crate. Mare unlatched Wookie's crate door and his eyes opened. Barreling out to visit, I dug fingers into his coat and kissed his muzzle. Wookie's markings were similar to Noah's, but his features were not as soft. Growls from each brother indicated the visit would not last long.

The sun dawned Thursday on hundreds of Malamutes already out for their morning walks. Weight-pulling competition started at 9 a.m., and we needed to weigh in prior to that. Because he had only been practicing a few weeks, Noah was entered in the novice class.

We still had a few minutes before the event, and I walked Noah over to a young bitch he had been eying. Both Malamutes on lead, they flirted and played together. Noticing the shiny red harness, Icy's human companion asked about Noah's chances. I was unsure how he would do, and said, "He's an expert at getting distracted so it's going to be interesting. How about her?"

"She's not as seasoned as many of the others she's competing against, but you have to start somewhere."

Indeed.

We wished each other luck, and she continued on to the conformational event inside with Icy.

Noah's name was called, and I brought him over to the pavement. Once attached to the cart holding four hundred pounds of dog food, he would have forty-five seconds to pull the load sixteen feet. I took my place at the other end where a crossing line had been taped to the asphalt. Unsure what would happen next, I called him. Effortlessly, Noah began walking towards me with the cart in tow, completing the distance in eleven seconds.

"Good boy! Good Noah!"

The next round, three more bags of dog food were added to the cart. Noah dug his back legs into the pavement, easily pulling five hundred and twenty pounds in just nine seconds. He had the hang of this.

Round three underway and he was harnessed to a six hundred and forty-pound load. A crowd was starting to build as eliminations from the conformational event came over to watch. Walking to the other end of the tape, I was confident Noah would pull over a thousand pounds today.

"Noah… Come!"

He remained motionless.

"Noah, c'mon buddy!"

Dang, he wasn't even trying.

"Noah. Hey... Noah!"

Completely inattentive to me, his gaze was fixed on the cute little bitch he had been introduced to earlier. Noah was finished pulling and eager to play again.

Our final night in Carlisle, Shy, Sandy, Mare, and myself were together for dinner. We all would be going our separate ways in the morning. Listening as the three of them compared war stories from the conformational front, I was glad not to be involved in the politics of showing a dog.

The Alaskan Malamute Club of America's annual auction was held afterward, and each of us attended. Beautiful and rare items were placed up for bid and a few oddball things as well. The others won their auctions. Mare did especially well, winning the privilege to have Wookie featured in a future book by renowned dog author Susan Conant. I did not bid on anything. I had already won.

That evening, I presented Noah with his trophy. The inscription engraved on the brass plate reads:

1998 Alaskan Malamute Nationals
Malko's Never A Prisoner...
Always A Champion!

"You can't own a wolf any more than you can own a rainbow. You can't fit a wolf into your domesticated world any more than you could fit the Northern Lights into your living room."

Never A Prisoner

I credit my father for my capacity to love and respect animals. Not just dogs, but all living creatures. Having gained from him an appreciation of nature few others seem to share, the human callousness I witness toward wildlife is appalling.

One nightmare in particular from my youth continues to haunt me. I had stopped by a neighbor's house to see if friends could play. Their mother answered the door and let me know that both boys were working in the garage with their father, but I could ask. I walked to the garage door and peeked through the window. On the other side of the glass, I could see them both, covered in blood, skinning rabbits along with their father. Never having seen death before, this premeditated slaughter of beautiful creatures—ones which I derived so much pleasure from watching in the field behind our house—was revolting. Sickened and confused, I ran home to my dad for an explanation. Answers would not come until the following year.

Every autumn, my father would hunt geese, and he began taking me along with him. We would walk for hours through fields and along streams, watching flocks fly overhead. All those years and dad did not fire a single shot, never once even raising his gun to the sky. Our time was spent looking at and listening to the natural world around us. The gun was a prop and hunting merely an excuse to get us out of the house. While we always came back home empty-handed, we were far richer in experience.

Nature can be appreciated fully only when it is left undisturbed. Too many times man tries to lay claim on things he can never control. Wolf hybrids are just one example of man attempting to domesticate nature.

Often referred to as a "wolf on a leash" because of their appearance, Alaskan Malamutes are not any more genetically related to wolves than are poodles or chihuahuas. All are members of *Canis lupus familiaris*. Sometimes people will crossbreed an Alaskan Malamute with a wolf, and their offspring are called Hybrids.

Humans are often fascinated with the wild. Its allure is largely because it is uncontrollable. Unfortunately, when one grasps at those things in nature, not only do they come up empty-handed, but often end up destroying it in the process.

Scoop up a handful of snow and examine the flakes. Each is beautiful and unique in its crystalline pattern. Bring one inside your home, and you're left with nothing more than a drop of water in your palm—a drop indistinguishable from any other drop of water. You must leave the snowflake outside in its natural environment to appreciate its beauty. I too am a wolf lover, but bringing one into my home would leave me with nothing but an unpredictable (and thus dangerous) canine.

For those who are compelled to have a wolf, they are there to enjoy freely in the wild. If you desire to live with wolves, do it on their terms. Join them in the wilderness and maybe they might even tolerate you. Don't think for a minute though that you can own a wolf. You can't own a wolf any more than you can own a rainbow. You can't fit a wolf into your domesticated world any more than you could fit the Northern Lights into your living room.

Noah had become my constant companion, and others began to notice. Family and coworkers expressed concern. Their worries, varied and insignificant, amounted to nothing more than ignorance of the breed. Many asked, "What about all that shedding?"

I assured all Alaskan Malamutes do not shed, they blow coat. While many breeds of dog lose some fur, a Malamute's undercoat literally explodes out of them—twice a year. There is no big secret to staying on top of all that hair. Brush them daily, and keep a good vacuum handy.

Others were troubled by the amount of noise a large dog might make, yet neighbors never complained about barking. One complete stranger mentioned about a surgical "fix" that was performed on her own dog. I know little about the de-barking procedure or medical ramifications of it. Dogs that bark incessantly are annoying to all, but in their defense, the most likely reason a dog barks for hours on end is boredom—because they have been neglected or ignored. This is not the fault of the dog, and blame lies solely with the owner.

Malamutes rarely bark, but I loved the sound of Noah's voice when he did. Just like his markings, scent, and personality, his voice was part of what defined him as "Noah." I have recorded his voice onto my answering machine, and have sound files of it on my computer. Dogs are with us for such a short period of time. I knew there would come a day when he would be forcefully ripped from my life, and I would no longer be able to hear his "woo woo." I do not know what it costs to silence a dog's voice. Were it possible, I would pay a thousand times that amount to always hear Noah's.

My world revolved around Noah, and many suggested that our relationship was unhealthy.

I am often asked, "How much does your dog mean to you?" Certainly, I care for Noah and see to it his physical and emotional needs are satisfied. This includes fresh water to drink and a high quality food for good health and energy. Just like humans, he needs to relieve himself and must be taken outside to do so. He requires a great deal of exercise, and we run together daily. Mental stimulation is provided through challenging games we play and food-oriented puzzles.

I love Noah. I put his physical and emotional needs before my own. If there were only food enough for one, he would get to eat. I would not hesitate to give my life up for him—I guess in no small part I already have. That may sound extreme to those who believe he is only a dog and, to most, he never will be anything more than just a dog.

Noah is my family, and I am fortunate to have him. A mother throws herself into traffic to save her child, and I won't hesitate to step in front of a car if it means sparing him. But then again, that is what love is—the sacrificing of self. Sacrificing one's own needs for the needs of another—not just some gushy emotion.

Love is a beautiful word. But to an Alaskan Malamute, words don't matter. Love as an action is dynamic. Actions are important. I can tell Noah I love him, verbally reminding him every day, but he will never understand. When I feed him, groom him, play with him, give him attention—only then he is able to comprehend.

Yes, I love him. It may sound extreme, but I don't believe one can ever love too much. It is possible a person might not love someone enough or may love another more. But one can never love too much. The absence of love is what causes problems.

So I am back to the question, "How much does your dog mean to you?" I will try to answer. Noah means as much to me as fireflies or the sound of crickets on a warm summer night. He means as much as a beautiful sunset casting its last rays on a frozen mountain peak. He is like the first snowfall, a warm summer's rain, the scent of cedar. He is my shooting star, my rainbow's end.

An intense bond between humans and dogs is not unique. "My New Boy," by Joan Phillips, is a children's story about a boy who thinks he is getting a new puppy, and a puppy that thinks he is getting a new boy. The puppy starts to take care of his boy right away, helping him eat dinner (taking the table scraps) and cleaning him (licking). He teaches his boy how to play tug of war and to throw a ball, but soon realizes his boy is not good at everything—he cannot dig very fast or run as quickly as he can. One day while out playing together, the puppy runs off. When he looks back, he doesn't see his boy anywhere. He wonders if his boy is lost and begins to look everywhere for him. Finally (at the end of the story), he sees his boy. The boy sees his puppy too and is glad to be reunited. "Woof! Woof! Woof! I tell my boy he must not get lost again."

My strong attachment to Noah, while inevitable, was not unusual. The Associated Press released a story on March 1, 1999, about a missing boy.

NORTON, Mass.—The body of a 9-year-old boy who disappeared looking for his dog in a snowstorm was found yesterday by a shallow stream about 300 yards from his family's home. The body of Cory Anderson was found curled in a ball in underbrush along an icy brook after the stripes from his Boston Bruins jacket caught a searcher's eye, police said. Cory was dressed warmly, wearing two jackets, a sweater, and fur-lined boots when he left his house Thursday in a storm that dumped 7 inches of snow in the area. He was looking for Jasmine, a golden retriever mix who had bolted from the house earlier. The dog turned up an hour later in a neighbor's yard.

A child, with complete disregard for his own safety, gave his life looking for his dog. While others sympathize for Cory's parents, my heart goes out to Jasmine, who has lost her boy. Hopefully, she will find another boy to play with and love. I would like to believe Cory's days are spent in an eternal winter wonderland filled with snow, his nights lit by Northern Lights. I am certain there is an Alaskan Malamute with him by his side, wherever he goes.

Noah turned heads wherever we went, and people used all sorts of words to describe him. Stunning. Beautiful. Magnificent. We would get many requests when out. Some asked to have a picture taken with him. Others wanted to know if it is all right to feed him a treat (the answer to that one was always a firm no). The most common request—to pet him—was one we were always willing to grant.

The strangest appeal came from an eight-year-old girl. She spotted us walking and ran over. Out of breath, she asked if she could have Noah's collar. I explained that Noah needs a collar in case he was ever lost, and pressed her for a reason why. She responded simply, "To wear it."

I pressed for further explanation.

"I'm going to marry him."

"Ah, and the collar will serve as some sort of engagement trinket." I wondered out loud, "Do your parents know?"

Nodding yes, she pleaded again for it. I made a temporary collar for Noah with the lead and removed his tags before handing her the black choker. She slipped the collar past her ears and smiled. Noah gave her a quick lick on the face before we continued on. There was a spare collar at home.

> Noah wears a collar every time we go out. There are three tags attached to it by S-rings. When he moves, they jingle and sound like a miniature set of wind chimes. Holding his collar in my hands, I sit in front of him explaining what each is for.
>
> "Heart-shaped and red, this first tag is your rabies tag. It sports a date at the top followed by our vet's contact information. Having that information is nice because it tells others where to take you for medical help in case you are ever hurt or injured. All dogs are required to have a rabies shot

because this disease is communicable to humans. Now, I've had you immunized against other nasty things as well, such as parvovirus, kennel cough, and distemper, but this tag is proof of inoculation against rabies, and it is needed before this next one can be issued."

Oblong and silver, it is stamped with:

N.Y.S. AGR&MKTS
ALBANY, N.Y.
3495918

"Believe it or not, you've got to be licensed in New York State to be a dog. People don't need to be licensed to be human, so I guess that makes dogs special.

"The third tag is important and is engraved on both sides with information. One side reads:

MY NAME IS
-NOAH-
NEVER A PRISONER

"In case you are lost, people will know to call you Noah. Otherwise, they might dub you with some silly name like Fluffy or Pooch. The other side is inscribed with the word "REWARD" and has our phone number listed below. This way people can contact me, I will come for you, and we will be together again. Side by side like we are right now. Right where you belong."

Even with sweat dripping from my brow under the summer sun, I could always see snowfall reflected in his eyes. Many times it seemed to me that he was almost human. He understood that I am not quite canine. Late one night I was awakened to the sound of Noah howling. Never having heard him vocalize like that before, I was troubled.

"Are you feeling alright, Goofball?"

I looked him over; nothing was physically wrong. Walking back to the bedroom, Noah was on my heels and jumped on the bed. Pawing the sheets, he let out a low grumble and then a loud "Woo!"

I was no longer concerned at this point with him rousing my neighbors but worried instead that he might wake the dead. I walked back to the other room for a look around. The curtains were still open and light from the full moon illuminated the floor. It was obvious now why he was howling, and Luna's frosty glow was all the excuse he needed for us to go out and play. I looked at him while lacing up my boots. He started in again with the "woo woos," reminding me that he would always be a Malamute—telling me that he is Never A Prisoner!

Every autumn clocks are set back an hour as society returns to standard time. Fall Back and Spring Ahead. Spring is rough because an hour of the weekend just disappears. I have never minded setting my clock back sixty minutes in the autumn, though, as I equate it with an additional hour of sleep. Noah never saw it this way.

I rarely go out, but knowing there was an extra hour the next morning, I decided to visit with some old friends. I ran Noah and wore him out good. He was asleep in his crate before I snuck out. Returning home late that evening (or early that morning, depending on how you look at it), I let Noah out to go potty, set my clock back an hour and went to bed. Shortly thereafter, I was awakened by a ninety-pound furball standing over me. Turning my head to look at the clock, a stream of saliva hit me on the cheek, and I wiped it off with the wolf-printed pillowcase.

"Go lay down—I still have another hour of sleep."

Undeterred, he let out a low grumble and began pawing at me to get up. Realizing the futility at this point of trying to sleep, I dressed and headed to the kitchen. An Alaskan Malamute's perception of time is different than a human's. Instead of looking at setting the clock back as gaining an hour of sleep, Noah perceived it as losing an hour of food—and he would not be cheated.

On Thanksgiving Day, an editorial was published in the local paper describing what I was thankful for:

> Many people hold special and will celebrate specific dates during the year. They call them holidays. I think the pageantry of the holiday season is beautiful, and just because I don't partake in it does not mean I can't appreciate it. I won't be setting up a tree and decorating it with colored lights or hanging up stockings. But don't confuse this lack of pageantry with a lack of spirit. December 25th means no more to me than any other day arbitrarily picked out of the year—say, August 7th. It's not that I don't consider December 25th

special. On the contrary, I consider every day throughout the year to be special. When I wake up with Noah's face looking at me, every morning is Christmas morning. No gift under a tree could be more beautifully wrapped than my Alaskan Malamute is in his seal and white.

Thanksgiving draws to a close, and I most likely won't have had any turkey today. I didn't have any turkey on August 7th either. But I do have a happy and healthy dog. I don't need a specific day or food to be thankful. I am reminded every day of my blessings, and I am thankful every night for them—as I lay down to sleep and I feel Noah's heart beat next to mine.

During that holiday season, one shopping mall advertised a photographer set up inside to take Christmas pictures of pets. It would be nice to have Noah's picture taken with "Santa Claws." Early that morning, I brushed out his coat and trim his paws. It began to snow when we arrived at the mall, the large white flakes adding to the festive atmosphere. Inside, we walked down the long corridors of shops. I was used to all the attention Noah garnered when we were out. There was no line, and I breathed a sigh of relief. We would not have to wait for a picture with Santa Claws. I was initially reluctant to bring him. He was great around most dogs, but his strong predatory reaction to cats concerned me.

I handed a twenty-dollar bill to one of the elf-dressed assistants. Eager to greet Santa, Noah could smell a collection of treats in the pocket of his red jacket.

I positioned my boy in front of the bearded old man and tried drawing his attention toward the camera. With a flash of the bulb, it was over. It appears we might get through this without incident.

"C'mon, buddy."

Placing his front paws on my shoulders, Noah licked my face. Reaching into my pocket, I drew out a biscuit to reward his exemplary behavior. The treat was quickly devoured. Punching both paws flat on the floor, his butt went high and his tail started wagging.

"Oh, no," I groaned, recognizing the sign that foreshadowed his break with reality.

Possessed, Noah began to rip around in circles. Santa Claws stood to take cover behind his chair while stunned elves cowered behind photographic equipment. I tried to settle Noah down but it was too late. Crazy Malamute had seized control of his mind. Holiday-themed picture frames flew in the air and snow globes crashed to the floor. I grasped his mug shot and grabbed hold of the lead. Pulling him in my direction, we made a beeline for the exit. Not without incident after all, but we had our print.

Others look at photos of Noah and see pictures. When I view these same images, I perceive memories and can clearly envision what each moment was like. A winter scene of him in the snow, I can feel the cold. Others left only to imagine, I remember. Noah and I were always busy doing something—busy making memories.

There had been times last year, on long treks with Noah, when the cotton and acrylic coat I wore that was so comfortable during cool autumn days just was not capable of keeping me warm in the middle of winter. I was not going to make the same mistake again and ordered a down coat from Mountain Gear. The company carries a vast supply of clothing and equipment specifically designed for extreme outdoor conditions. Technical gear is expensive, but well worth the cost when one considers frostbite and freezing to death.

My coat arrived via UPS a few days after placing the order. I signed for the package and rushed back inside with my prize—a 650-fill down coat in cobalt blue by Mountain Hardware. It fit perfectly. Incredibly light and warm, it would retain body heat even on the coldest of days. Not wanting my new coat to smell like a smoky bar, I laid it on the bed and gave Noah a kiss on his black strip. I told him to be good and left for work.

I returned home that evening expecting the usual but realized something was amiss when I opened the door. Noah did not greet me at the entrance, and there was an odd white fluff strewn across the floor. He had gotten into something, most likely destroying one of his toys and spending the afternoon ripping out its fluffy guts. Still, it was everywhere and difficult to imagine any toy of his having this amount of stuff inside. I bent down and scooped up a handful. This was not ordinary stuffing used to fill toys. Rather, these were goose-down feathers used to fill... I rushed to the bedroom. Lying on top of the bed, Noah chewed on a piece of cobalt-blue cloth pausing just long enough to greet me. "Woo woo."

I called Mountain Gear again. My name must have rung a bell, because the woman on the other end remarked that she had sold me an identical down coat just a few days ago.

"Yeah, I just recently ordered a cobalt-blue jacket, but this order is for garnet red." Not that the color of a down coat would ever make any difference to a Malamute.

Throughout his life, there were two things Noah would never experience. First, he would never know what it is like to be satiated. Malamutes have an efficient metabolism and are capable of tremendous amounts of work on restricted diets. Food is scarce and competition for calories high in the barren lands from which they originated. A survival mechanism, their brains are hardwired so they are constantly hungry. Noah would never know the feeling of a full stomach, and because of his dual coat, he would never be cold. I kept my down coat in the closet from then on, when I'm not wearing it. I did not foresee being cold again, either.

My down coat had been destroyed in a vicious fit of boredom and it would only be a matter of time before something else was too. I thought it best to crate Noah when I was gone. People have mixed feelings about crating dogs, and some consider it cruel. Done properly, it is not abusive, and I am sure Noah would have agreed. He spent six hours a day in his crate while I was at work. It was comfortable, with padding underneath a folded bed sheet and it was fully stocked with his favorite toys. He was thoroughly exercised before I put him in each afternoon. When I was home the crate door was left open. Often, he would be inside, lying on his back, paws in the air and tongue hanging out.

He has never been forced into his crate and always entered willingly. People argue that it is not fair to a dog, that they are unhappy when confined like this. Many people equate happiness with a certain amount of success, and Noah was no different.

Success comes in many a guise. Most only

recognize it in the familiar forms of money, fame, or love. What success is to one may be something completely different to another. Noah equated prosperity with food, and this is his secret to success:

Noah was always fed in his crate.

Success requires one to be in the right place at the right time.

Since Noah never knew exactly when the right time is going to be, he figured that the trick was to just find the right place and hang around. If the right place happened to be in his crate, he would happily chew on a bone while waiting for dinner.

Noah taught me all I need to know about success. I can do without a sports car, fancy gold jewelry, or expensive trip. Prosperity really only requires a bowl of food, a place to call home, and a faithful companion.

"I tried prying his mouth open, but this action elicited only a low growl, and his jaws remained tightly shut. I pulled on the brush. Thinking we now were playing a game of tug, he resisted and began pulling back. Suddenly, the toothbrush snapped, and Noah just as quickly swallowed the bristled end."

Snowdog

Canines need regular physical examinations and medical treatment as much as humans do. Choosing the right veterinarian was not a decision I was taking lightly, knowing this person would become a partner in Noah's life and play an active role in his well-being. My ideal vet not only renders emergency medical care, but also provides necessary preventative services essential for good health. I interviewed several veterinarians, including their office staff and their clients, before deciding on one I felt was best for us.

Preventative care services offered by most veterinary practices include wellness exams, vaccinations, and heartworm checks. While grooming Noah daily allowed me the opportunity to physically examine him, yearly wellness visits provided a professional evaluation of overall health. Vaccinations were also administered during this exam, including shots for rabies, distemper, parvovirus, and kennel cough.

Yearly heartworm testing was not something on which I agree with our vet. Noah received heartworm meds year-round, so I feel it is unnecessary. The bulk of a veterinary practice's income is derived from preventative care services, though. I understand this and have no problem until I was pressured to subject Noah to a stressful procedure (like drawing blood) with no purpose other than to help fill the till.

Just like humans, Noah was susceptible to gum disease and tooth decay. Unlike us, he does not readily spit things out. He figured that what fit in his mouth must be food. This applies to toothpaste as well, but the fluoride it contains is not necessarily something good for him to ingest. Fortunately, there is a canine alternative, and turkey-flavored toothpaste can be purchased from almost any vet. The directions on the package make it sound easy to use: Apply a small amount on a toothbrush and gently brush over teeth. While I consider it a necessary preventative procedure, it is anything but easy to accomplish with an Alaskan Malamute.

The first time I brought a tube of this turkey toothpaste home, I forgot to buy a second toothbrush and ended up using my own. Noah was immediately attracted to the poultry odor. This would be a cinch, I mistakenly thought. Enjoying the taste of toothpaste so much, he would not let go of the toothbrush and held it firmly between his back molars—the same ones he uses to grind bones with. A stern "leave it" had no effect. I tried prying his mouth open, but this action elicited only a low growl, and his jaws remained tightly shut. I pulled on the brush. Thinking we now were playing a game of tug, he resisted and began pulling back. Suddenly, the toothbrush snapped, and Noah just as quickly swallowed the bristled end. Three days and one barium X-ray later, Noah finally eliminated the missing section of my toothbrush. The incident did not deter me from his dental care. From then on, I applied the turkey toothpaste to a gauze pad wrapped around my finger and brushed his teeth this way. The large size of my fist between his jaws prevented him from taking my finger off the way he took off the handle of the brush.

Some dogs have a difficult time at the vet's office. Not every appointment with Noah was easy simply because of his typical Malamute personality. Strong-willed and having mastered the art of "selective listening," it is this fierce independence that has allowed Alaskan Malamutes to survive in the cold harsh climate in which they originated. Newcomers can quickly find themselves in over their heads without first understanding how a snow dog is different from other more "domesticated" breeds. Rescues and reputable breeders prefer that only those experienced with headstrong dogs bring a Malamute into their lives. The flip side of all this is a well-adjusted, socialized Malamute that understands his or her place in the world—a free-spirited goofball living in the moment.

All it took for Noah to comply was a bit of tasty bribery. A small biscuit or treat sufficed, and he gladly expended a hundred calories for a ten-calorie reward. There were occasions however when even a Thanksgiving dinner would not convince him my bidding was in his best interest. This clash of wills between human and Malamute is epic in proportion—the canine equivalent of a showdown at the O. K. Corral.

Noah was indifferent to veterinary visits until four years old. I thought there might be a problem when I saw him scoot his back end on the ground. I can think of no other way to describe it other than lifting his tail up, planting his butt on the ground, and with his back legs in the air, pulling himself forward with both front paws. Maybe it was just an itch or piece of poop he was trying to scrape off, but the scooting lasted for a few seconds and then stopped.

The next morning, he was scooting again. Too coincidental to be another piece of stuck poop, I was clueless to the cause. When he started dragging his butt again after dinner, I knew there was a problem. We returned home, and I made a vet appointment.

Noah was scooting because of impacted anal glands. These two small sacs are located just inside the anus, their viscous material the foulest-smelling stuff imaginable. Most wild animals empty their sacs voluntarily and often do so to mark territory. Malamutes normally void them each time they defecate. Unable to voluntarily empty his sacs, Noah's glands became impacted and uncomfortable. He was scooting for relief. Left untreated, an abscess usually forms and can be very painful when it ruptures.

I was informed Noah's sacs would need to be voided for him. Meanwhile, he had become extremely protective of his back end, growling each time his tail was lifted. A muzzle was necessary to keep everyone safe. Wrapping my arms around his chest, I pressed my head against his neck. The technician placed both arms under his belly to prevent him from dropping his back end. Noah let out a muffled shriek and stiffened as a finger was inserted into his rectum. He was not happy with this turn of events and struggled violently while the vet expressed each gland. The small exam room smelled putrid, with all of us drenched in sweat and anal stink from this one-minute ordeal. I cautiously removed the muzzle, and surprisingly, Noah just sat there. Not so surprisingly, he was waiting for a treat.

A dozen roses were later delivered to the veterinary office, and I included a note apologizing for Noah's behavior and thanking the entire staff for their part in making my dog well again.

"A tired Malamute is a good Malamute."

24 Paws in the Morning

After thirteen years in the same two-bedroom apartment, my lease was not renewed. I was offered a one-bedroom instead. These government-subsidized units had a waiting list of low-income families and the landlord was mandated to offer multiple bedroom units to them first. I had an Alaskan Malamute larger than most children. Legally, though, we were still considered just a single person on the lease.

Many special occasions had taken place in my apartment and I was initially reluctant to move. But Noah had quietly been teaching me memories are not contained between walls and any given place is merely a shell in which wonderful moments are born. Home is nothing more than where we bed down for the night. Many times it was that apartment, but occasionally it has been a log cabin in Pennsylvania. Often, home was somewhere on the trail in the middle of the night.

Trepidation gave way to anticipation as I considered a different floor plan with new carpet and a fresh coat of paint. The basement unit was literally next door to the one I was moving out of. No truck or van required. I would walk down a flight of stairs and out the door, turn right, walk twenty feet and down a few steps into my new place.

The biggest difference between apartments was a large window at ground level instead of a sliding glass door with a balcony. Noah would miss the balcony so a plan was hatched for his new kennel. The ground window would serve as a doggie door that a wooden ramp in the living room angled up to. Just outside, I planned on covering the ground with patio blocks and fencing in a four by ten foot area with chain link. The most difficult challenge proved to be moving those six cement blocks and at one hundred and twenty pounds each, I could only load two at a time in the car. Being a renter, I lacked many of the tools most homeowners take for granted, including a wheelbarrow. Forced to carry each block eighty feet from where I parked on the side of the road, I worked to exhaustion. But when the job was done, Noah could run up the ramp and out the window to his own private area. There, safe in his den, he spent hours watching the world unfold.

Meanwhile, Shy and I were slowly testing the boundaries of our friendship. Living now in a mobile home just outside the small town of Cochranton, she was having serious problems with her current flame. Whether or not she and I could pick up from where we had left off two years earlier was something yet to be discovered. But, ready to find out, Noah and I drove to Pennsylvania for the weekend, and I booked two nights at a motel in nearby Meadville.

We arrived Friday afternoon and settled into our room with plenty of time to kill. Unable to get time off, Shy was still at work and would need to put in a full day again tomorrow as well. I turned the television on and left Noah atop the bed with a knucklebone. That would buy me some time for a quick drive around town to reacquaint myself with memories of a past I thought forever lost.

Memories are a selective recollection of past events often reinforced by the familiarity of a location, scent, or sound that sometimes trigger an emotional response. They are the byproduct of now, like exhaust from an engine, fueled by the opportunities of the future.

That evening, a knock at the door startled Noah. Jumping off the bed, he shot me his desperate "hurry up and get it" look. A familiar woman walked in carrying a bag of wrapped gifts, presents she had never gotten around to delivering at Christmas. I had not seen her since the '98 Nationals, a year and a half earlier. The only noticeable change was a shorter hairstyle.

But short locks were not fooling Noah. Immediately recognizing Shy, he was on her, pausing just long enough to race around the room before wetting her face again with kisses. With Noah's help, I opened the gifts and let him keep the wrapping paper to tear up at leisure while Shy and I stepped out for dinner.

> There is no big secret to leaving an Alaskan Malamute alone in a hotel room. Noah and I live harmoniously in a small apartment because he is afforded both physical exercise and mental stimulation. Letting a dog out to "run and play" is not enough.

Run together. A three-mile run will wear a Malamute out for several hours, and the exercise is good for their human companion as well. The destructive power of a bored Malamute rivals that of any natural disaster, except that it is contained within four walls. A tired Malamute is a good Malamute.

The next morning, Noah and I drove to see Shy's mom in Erie. Susie always enjoys these visits, and Noah was happy for the opportunity to run loose in the yard. Though she was too polite to ask, I could tell she is curious about her daughter's relationships. I could not provide an answer, instead sharing only that of which I was certain—we were going out later that evening.

Shy stopped by the room shortly before sunset to quickly give me the game plan. We were meeting up with two of her close friends for a few drinks and to watch a local band. She still needed to feed her dogs, but would be back soon. An evening of pizza, beer, and rock 'n'roll with a pretty blonde on one's arm has all the makings of a good time, and I was not disappointed.

Shy returned me to the hotel well past midnight. I was leaving early in the morning, yet she insisted on seeing me once more over breakfast. There were a few hours of sleep remaining before we were together again over coffee. Still unsure of where things were headed, Noah and I both kissed Shy and departed for home. We planned to visit again in a few weeks.

Shy ended the relationship with her boyfriend, and this time Noah and I were staying with her. The yellow mobile home, not nearly as dingy as described, was on a dirt road well into farm country. Having come from a beautiful log cabin though, I understood why she considered this place inferior. Kennels set up in back, the yard was fenced in from pasture bordering each side. Horses and cows were grazing across the road.

Familiar faces peer out from the kennels. Erika, Taylor, and Maija began pacing back and forth. Erika appears thinner than I remember. Taylor and Maija are stunning in their full coats. Venerable 'Tica and Kochise have slowed down considerably. Chanco and Cheyenne were not here, having remained at the cabin with her ex-husband when he took possession.

Shy walked out to greet me and tried to visit with Noah. But, uninterested in human affection right now, he preferred to investigate the new surroundings. I let him sniff around for a few minutes before kenneling him between Erika and Maija.

Only the absence of log walls indicated that it was a different home. The interior was filled with wolf sculptures and prints from Shy's cabin, taking up every inch of available space. Shy would need to be up early for work so, after going out for Italian, we called it an evening.

It was still dark when the alarm went off. Shy showered and then fed the dogs.

It's 5 a.m. in Western Pennsylvania, and six hungry Malamutes are impatiently waiting to be fed.

A cup and a half of Eukanuba for Noah. Two cups for Erika. Maija and Taylor each get one. One cup also for Kantica and Kochise.

Maija is first out. She makes her way

down the steps and circles the yard, sniffing for a good spot to go potty. Still half asleep, I walk with her to the kennels. She occupies the farthest one from the gate. FILO is the rule with Alaskan Malamutes—First In, Last Out. Preventing them from walking past each other minimizes the risk of confrontation. *Never Say Never*. Many times it is only because of FILO that two bitches like Taylor and Erika don't rip at each other's throats.

I let Noah out next. Lifting a hind leg, he begins marking territory along the fence. He sees me walking toward the kennels. Knowing his time is limited, he bolts around the yard in circles. He is *Never A Prisoner*. I start to run and Noah chases after me. In the darkness, I trip in one of the holes that have been dug in the yard. Within seconds he is on me, licking my face. I love my boy and believe sometimes he loves me too.

I kennel Noah next to Maija before walking back to get Taylor. The sky is just starting to redden in the East with the coming of daybreak. I unlatch the crate door, and like a silver rocket, she is out in a flash. I stand in awe, watching as she runs through the dawn. It is breathtaking to watch her move. Taylor goes potty and then grabs a chunk of grass and dirt. I hear Erika's impatient "woo woo" from inside the house and know it's time to kennel

Taylor—but not before she can plant a muddy kiss.

Erika is vocal and makes it clear she wants out. Quickly down the steps, first to go potty and then four paws on a dime. The mud she's eaten yesterday has finally made its way to her other end. When finished, Erika runs to me, forcefully thrusting her front paws into my chest. She then turns around and sprints toward the kennels where Noah is anxiously awaiting to visit. Knowing two Malamutes are still crossing their legs inside, I am careful this crafty bitch isn't afforded any opportunity for trouble. *Always A Princess.*

Dew on the grass becomes evident as the sky brightens. 'Tica and 'Chise gingerly descend the steps and potty. Slowly making their way together, they occupy the kennel closest to the gate.

I walk back to the house as the sun begins to rise.

Shy left for work and would not return until that afternoon. I spent time with each Malamute and drove into town for groceries and hardware supplies so I could perform some necessary repairs around the house. Shy returned to a steak dinner, and we spent the evening watching a movie.

The next morning, I snapped several pictures of Malamutes before Noah and I depart. I hoped for one of Shy, too, but it is a rarely granted request. Just before leaving, however, she allows one picture of her—wrapped in a wolf blanket—standing at the top of her drive.

More than a month passes before we could see each other again. I was excited about this visit, hoping to learn where our relationship was headed. Shy had the weekend off, allowing us much more time together.

Entertainment began immediately. Not out of the car yet, I watched as the neighbor's filly bolted through pasture bordering the kennels. Kenneled Malamutes howled like a three-alarm fires in progress. Noah was trying to get to the scene through the Camaro's windshield. Then followed fifteen minutes of chasing the mare until we could get her back across the road and into her stall.

It proved to be a harbinger of things to come. What had begun with promise and adventure quickly deteriorated as it became painfully obvious we were moving in separate directions. While differences in a relationship many times can allow people room to grow closer together, ever-expanding gaps eventually become unbridgeable. Conceding that we were unable to recapture the past, I had no desire to compete for Shy's future.

Noah and I returned home to the promise of other possibilities. What those possibilities were, I had no idea but would soon find out. I had faith that someone wonderful could walk into my life at any moment.

"If one is ever to think like an Alaskan Malamute, one must learn first to see like one."

Faith

Each morning after he ate, Noah accompanied me on a long run. Our timing coincided with the morning commute, and many of those on their way to work wave as they pass us. Michelle is one of these people and she occasionally stops to pet Noah. Upon discovering that I was unattached, she insisted on introducing me to her single friend. But, all sweaty, I did not need to be acquainted with anything other than a bar of soap at that moment.

Three miles later, Noah rode with me to the gym. He chewed on a bone while waiting in the backseat of the car. There was a regular morning crew that met there each morning. We had gotten to know each other fairly well and one of the ladies, Ruth, mentioned that her sister was single. While I was keeping my options open, jumping blind into another relationship was not in my plans.

Where does one go in search of a companion - someone to talk with and enjoy life's moments together? Some find that special person in their church. Other times a relationship develops between co-workers. Many people go to bars. Well, I do not go to church and dating a co-worker is out of the question—a bar is the last place I want to be after working in one all day. I turned to the same place I had found success previously—online.

The underlying theme amongst most people looking for a relationship online is that they are unloved and want someone else to fill in the gaps. That they are "halves" looking for another half to complete them. Whatever holes might have existed in my life, Noah filled. I desired a complete person I could share life and experiences with. Because I was not looking for a "half," my search quickly narrowed to just one person.

Faith listed a personal ad online at her friend Connie's request. Quickly sorting through hundreds of profiles, hers was the only one I responded to. I replied with a brief description and my interests. I did not include a picture of myself, instead attaching one of Noah. She responded back and that began an e-mail exchange. Soon after, we began talking nightly. We arranged to meet one Friday night after work. She was going to be at a local bar with friends and asked if I would like to join them. Anxious to meet this woman who had so quickly attracted me, I agreed.

Our first date suffered a major setback when Faith changed the meeting location and neglected to tell me. I showed up to the agreed-upon place on time and found no one matching her description. Finishing my beer, I went home to Noah. The phone rang a short while later. It was Faith calling—wanting to know if I was standing her up. Certainly not, but I had no desire to go back out again either.

We made plans to try and meet again a few days later. This time we would meet at my apartment. Noah and I were waiting on the lawn when Faith parked her car. Something about the vehicle looked familiar. We talked for a bit and then went out to shoot a few games of pool. Over the next few weeks we continued to spend much of our time together. Typical dating stuff like dinners, movies, and long walks with Noah. That summer, the wonderful friendship we shared developed into an exclusive relationship.

Some meetings are destined to happen. I discovered a short while later that not only was she Michelle's best friend and Ruth's sister, but that she worked across the street from me—in fact, we had been parking in the same lot. The relationship appeared inevitable.

Many times in a new relationship, animal companions that have been with us all along get ignored. Not so with Noah. We continued to go on adventures, often with Faith and sometimes by ourselves. The Fireman's Carnival is an annual summer event that always kicks off with a parade. While the route was being set up, Noah and I walked past the uniformed participants, visiting with local fire departments and color guards. Noah posed for pictures on several fire engines and with one of the marching bands. We were asked to march with the group and, while an honor, it was too warm that day to be walking several miles on asphalt with an Alaskan Malamute. We returned home and Noah spends the remainder of the evening in his kennel chewing on ice cubes and watching fireflies, fascinated by these bugs that light up.

Noah will let me know when something is out of the ordinary. If we are walking and come across an orange construction cone that was not there the day before, he will stop in his tracks and growl. Minutes later, when it becomes obvious the cone is not intimidated, he will slowly walk toward it to investigate.

Some nights it is too buggy, and I keep Noah inside with me. One such evening he is standing in the bathroom doorway, making all sorts of noise. I flicked on the light to see what all the commotion is about—a little brown bug perched on the shower curtain. I did not want it in the apartment, so I swatted the bug onto the porcelain surface, quickly squishing it with a ball of wadded up toilet paper. But instead of typical bug guts, neon goo smears across the tub, and I realize my terrible mistake. Noah had been calling me over to look at the bug with him. Instead of observing in the dark like he had been, I turned on the light and never saw its unmistakable glow. Had the bathroom light been on all along, Noah would not have paid any attention. The bug was only of interest to him when it was lighting up—in the dark. I learned an important lesson. If one is ever to think like an Alaskan Malamute, one must learn first to see like one.

Faith's love and compassion for animals was evident from the start. She had taken in a baby squirrel that had been abandoned on her back step, and trying to nurse him back to health. He was kept safe and warm in a small cage and fed numerous times each day with an eyedropper. A week passed and despite all of this care, his condition deteriorated. Faith called to let me know her squirrel was sick and I felt her frustration and helplessness. A short while later, the little gray squirrel died.

I met Faith for lunch, and she handed me a small box before returning to work. The sad design flaw with living creatures is their finite duration and inability to withstand significant deviation from a numerous set of parameters required to survive. Evolutionary theory prevents the intelligent from taking legal action against such Almighty incompetence. Gathering acorn seeds along the way to a nearby wooded area, I buried the baby squirrel beneath a maple tree.

Autumn was underway when I awoke one night extremely ill. Jumping up on the bed to check out the nocturnal activity, Noah licked my face. His tongue felt rather cool. Burning up with fever, I was suddenly overcome with a wave of nausea. Rushing to the bathroom, I fill the bucket with my stomach's contents and then call Faith. She was by my side within an hour.

That morning, Faith fed and walked Noah before taking me to a doctor. Diagnosed with the flu, I would be out of action for several days. But my Malamute was not going to understand or allow me any bedrest. Faith assures me all will be fine, however, and spends the week caring for Noah and I. Nursing others back to health seems intuitive to her.

By Halloween, I had recovered and looked forward to partaking in the festivities. Noah was always dressed for the occasion, brown eyes peering from behind his beautiful mask. An old crate sheet provided me with an excellent ghost costume. Faith came over dressed as a witch. It was difficult recognizing her from the wretched hag standing before me. Noah, however, was not fooled and easily saw beyond the spooky green makeup and black garb—she still smelled like Faith. The three of us greeted each costumed little one that came to the door and passed out candy from my Halloween "Boo Bag." Eventually Faith had to go home. But Noah and I have become fond of her companionship.

I have always enjoyed mountains. My father would take the family to the Adirondacks each summer. Much of the time we were in Saranac Lake, where we spent our days fishing and hiking in the wilderness. The entire region has an allure I wanted to share with Faith.

Shortly before Christmas, we decided to spend a weekend in Lake Placid. This trip would be a journey through my heart shared with my two closest friends—one a human named Faith, the other an Alaskan Malamute called Noah. Leaving Rochester, most others were scurrying to finish holiday shopping on their lunch break. It was already dark and snowing hard when we entered the mountains, the only view driving in of flakes rushing towards the windshield. Even in blackness, I could feel mountains around us.

Late that first evening, we arrived at Adirondack Lodge, a log cabin nestled between tall pines on the edge of the Mirror Lake. Our first floor room had a sliding glass door that opened up to the lake. I let Noah out the back to potty and noticed eight inches of snow had accumulated—and it was still falling. Tomorrow morning would be epic.

We awoke early to Noah systematically pulling off each blanket. I did not want to leave the comfort of the bed or warmth of Faith by my side, but a hungry Malamute is not easily ignored. I filled his bowl with kibble, dressing while he ate. Minutes later, we were out. Several more inches of snow had fallen in the night. Flakes sparkled like diamonds when the morning sun occasionally peeked out from behind the clouds. The lake was frozen over and stretched out before us. I let Noah off lead for a quick run. The Adirondack Mountains surrounded us, a barrier between this world and the one I had left behind hundreds of miles ago.

Back at the lodge, Faith and I formulated a game plan over bacon and eggs at the Black Bear, unique for the "Adirondack Birch Squirrel" mounted on its wall. First order of business was to take Noah back out on the lake for more fun in the snow. Reluctant at first, I assured Faith the ice was thick enough to support us. Clouds broke and the sun came out. We squinted, our eyes nothing more than slits. Reflecting off new snowfall, we were blinded by the brilliant cold light. Whiteface Mountain stood in the distance and against this sentinel monolith we posed for pictures.

Main Street in the village of Placid is a retail extravaganza for tourists. Faith enjoys window-shopping, and Noah happily greeted all strangers as they passed. After a long day, the three of us dozed off together, Noah at my feet and Faith by my side.

The mountains are full of adventure if one knows where to look. My brother taught at a local prep school in Placid and played guide for a day. Faith and I met up with Jimmy after another breakfast at The Black Bear. Noah remained back at the room watching TV and working on a bone while we spent the day trekking through the high peaks. Light snowfall covered fir and balsam, the mountain vista like a page torn from an Adirondack fairy tale.

Reality check—after watching television all afternoon, Noah was anxiously awaiting my return. Happy to see me, he treated our first few minutes together as though we were just reunited after years of separation. Chasing each other through motel hallways allowed me to wear him out before traveling around the lake for dinner at Jimmy's.

Just before heading home the next morning, we make a last stop at a souvenir shop. The cramped shack was filled with T-shirts, sweatshirts, glasses, mugs, keychains, magnets and silver spoons—all stamped with "Lake Placid." Displayed in a corner were wooden boxes, each with a different design carved into the lid. I took an immediate liking to one in particular—a cedar box with a wolf etched on top—and bought it.

A mist was rolling across Mirror Lake as we departed and the mountains were covered in clouds. No longer able to "see," I took comfort that I still could at least "know" of their beauty.

I listened to Noah behind me chewing on his bone while Faith drove. Holding the small box in my hands, tears flowed freely.

Faith looked over. "What do you plan on putting in it?"

Brass hinges allow me to part the lid from the box. Once again I am enveloped in the scent of cedar—the frozen peaks of Algonquin and Cascade... ice-covered lakes—and sharing it all with Faith and Noah.

"There's no room for anything more inside," I replied. "It's full of memories."

"I thought that any love is good love so I took what I could get. And then she looked at me with those big, brown eyes and said, 'You ain't seen nothin' yet!'" – Randy Bachman

Home Improvement

Shy had been living in a log cabin tending after eight Alaskan Malamutes and a Siberian Husky when we met. She did not have a job and showed many of her dogs each weekend. Her separation and subsequent divorce left her with little choice but to leave the life of a "princess" and become self-sufficient. She realized after two and a half years of working at Walmart that she was able to do little more than cover her bills.

Hoping to become financially secure in a professional line of work, she returned to school for certification as a radiological technician. Meeting the requirements for such a degree is rigorous and time-consuming. The plan was for her to leave Walmart, with her father helping with necessary expenses while she studied. Dad made it clear he did not consider Alaskan Malamutes a necessary expense, however. Had there been no conditions on his assistance, Shy would have accepted the offer and gone to school at least a year earlier. Her ex-husband had taken Chanco and

Cheyenne, but the five remaining Malamutes still required considerable money and care. Putting the interests of her dogs first, Shy was waiting for the best time to make a shuffle.

Kantica and Kochise were not doing well. Kantica could no longer see and depended upon her brother to lead her around. Kochise had problems of his own, with his hips causing him so much pain it was difficult for him to stand. Their quality of life was quickly deteriorating and their health failing. Shy made the difficult decision to put them down together. I am unable to comprehend the tremendous grief she felt carrying each dog to her car and then into the vet's office for that final visit. After Kantica and Kochise were unbound from their earthly existence, Shy carried their bodies back to her car and drove to have them cremated. A few hours later she left with their remains. Even in death, Shy insisted on dignity and respect for her dogs.

I often inquired about possibly taking Taylor, as I wanted a companion for Noah. Realizing this was an opportune time to part with her, Shy could not think of a more ideal placement. She called, and we made arrangements for a transfer.

I pulled up beside her Camaro in the agreed-upon parking lot. Taylor was in the front passenger seat watching me. Shy got out, her hair disheveled and mascara running. If she harbored any doubts about letting Taylor go, I was willing to take her on a temporary basis only. Too slow in verbalizing my thoughts, I was astonished by her sudden clairvoyance.

"This is definitely the right thing to do. She'll have a permanent home and finally get all the love she deserves. Yesterday I had to put ' Tica and 'Chise down. I haven't gotten any sleep yet."

I wrapped my arms around her. Holding her tight, I felt her chin pressed against my shoulder. "I am so sorry. Let me know if there is anything I can do. I'll love Taylor."

"I know you will."

While Shy said goodbye, I loaded the crate and belongings into the back of my car. Opening the passenger door, I motioned Taylor in.

"C'mon, pretty girl."

Unsure whether to stay with Shy or come with me, Taylor stood there looking bewildered. I tossed a small treat into the back seat, and her mind was immediately made up.

Mid-May and winter is returning a bit quicker than I would have imagined. I consider meteorologists on par with mediums and tarot readers, putting little faith in their prediction of sunny skies and warm temperatures. They do the best they can with the equipment they have and the myriad ways in which to analyze data, yet I find myself more than slightly amused at their prediction. I guess they don't know what I know. I foresee a blizzard—high winds, frigid nights, and a blanket of snow covering the ground.

The clear skies and warm, sunny weather are not for me. Keep your manicured lawns and flowers. Enjoy your cookouts and gatherings, swimming in your pools. My world is cold, a beautifully harsh place of snow and ice where the North Wind screams across permafrost. This is where Noah and I play. Where we eat and sleep. Here, we choose to live our lives. Taylor is coming to join us. Home improvement is definitely in order. *Ch. Malko's Home Improvement*, that is.

We were on our way home. Taylor would be staying with Faith temporarily, but I was bringing her to my apartment first for a few days so we could get reacquainted. Trying to put the puzzle of our lives together, Taylor was a piece that fit perfectly.

"Seldom in life one is ever offered the ideal solution to a problem and instead must choose between any of the available 'best' options."

Beauty Paws

It was a dream of mine to provide Noah with living conditions similar to what he had been afforded at Shy's. Each evening I promised one day he would have his own kennel (not like the existing makeshift one built out the back window of my apartment), a large yard, and another Malamute to play with.

Faith shared a similar vision, her future headed in the same direction. Planning on spending every day together—for the rest of our lives—we discussed marriage. While a wedding was not immediately forthcoming, we considered it merely a legal technicality and began looking for our home.

The first few places were older farmhouses, allegedly needing just a little work. Having renovated her current home, Faith is talented with a hammer, but some of the structures we saw should really ought to be razed. Trying to narrow our search, I suggested prospective homes be post-Civil War dwellings with a roof, electricity, and running water.

In the first month of autumn, Faith and I looked at a place in the country. The house and horse barn sat on several acres of land, with half fenced off for pasture. The surrounding farmland and cornfields are similar to the town I grew up in, and nothing like the suburbanized municipality it has become. Attraction to the rural charm was immediate and walking inside to meet with the realtor, I loudly proclaimed, "We'll take it!"

Six weeks later, Noah, Taylor, and I moved into our new home. Faith would not join us for another month until her house sold, and prior to her arrival with a bed, I slept on the floor each night. Dog crates were temporarily set up in the living room while the downstairs was finished with carpet and fresh paint.

I hoped to have kenneling up before winter and began work immediately. Envisioning three 10' x 10' x 6' kennels of chain-link fencing that sat on a graded concrete bottom, this layout would allow the greatest amount of flexibility in the future.

The concrete base was necessary before setting up any chain link. A contractor was coming over within a week to pour a 12' x 32' slab. The area needed to be dug 12 inches deep and filled partway with several tons of gravel beforehand. I divided the length into thirty-two foot long rows and then cut those into twelve sections of one-foot squares. Clueless as to the amount of time and effort digging would require, it became apparent when I tried to remove the first square. An hour later, once the first row had been cleared, I came to another realization: Unless I wanted a hill overlooking the kennels, something needed to be done with all the sod piling up. Hauling dirt squares to the edge of the property with Faith's pick-up truck, I then tossed them in the field.

(These mounds would eventually find use as our pumpkin patch.) Physically punishing work completed the task. Concrete was delivered, poured, and graded at a slight angle to create run-off and minimize areas of standing pee. Once dry, a coating was applied to prevent it from dusting up.

Setting up the chain link was easy, entailing nothing more than slipping pre-made 10' x 6' panels onto steel rods encased in the cement. Dog huts with cozy crate pads inside were placed in each kennel. While it would still be several years before a permanent roof was constructed, the kennels were ready for Noah and Taylor.

Neither Malamute was left unattended in the kennels for any length of time. Without a roof, direct sunlight and rain were my two biggest concerns. On sunny mornings, I hung tarps on the east side, moving them south and then west as the day progressed. Of course, during early summer, the sun is so high off the horizon that by midday, none of the tarps offered any shade. During those afternoons, Noah and Taylor were inside with the air conditioner running and something interesting on the TV.

There was little I could do to prevent them from getting soaked during a rainstorm other than to try to bring them inside before one occurs. I had never paid much attention to forecasts before and began checking the temperature, cloud cover, and weather radar hourly.

Cleaning kennels requires little more than scooping poop and hosing them out daily. With no roof, a good rain shower gets the concrete base "naturally" clean. During the winter, cleaning is even easier. Snow packs up sometimes as high as eighteen inches, and pee freezes on the ice below. As more snow falls, it creates a fresh white blanket for them to play on. On milder days, I break apart the pee-laden ice underneath and shovel out the chunks.

The lack of a roof and the subsequent stress it was causing began to take a toll on us. We rarely eat out, but one summer evening Faith decided she was too tired to cook anything and it would be a nice change. The sky was clear, and we were not planning to be gone longer than an hour, so the dogs were left in their kennels. But no sooner did we place our orders than dark clouds began to roll in. The local radar was clear of precipitation when we left, and no rain had been in the evening forecast. Just as dinner arrived, however, I noticed water drops on the car windshield. We quickly ate, paid the bill, and headed back. One mile from home, the sky blackened, and a torrential rain began to fall. Faith remarked the dogs might be in their huts. I did not share her optimism. Noah and Taylor were standing in the downpour, indifferent to their soaking, as we pulled into the driveway. I hurried each inside and toweled them off and the rain abruptly stopped. We needed a roof over the kennels just as much as the Malamutes did.

Money was tight while Faith finished school. We considered several inexpensive ideas but each had some kind of drawback. Seldom in life one is ever offered the ideal solution to a problem and instead must choose between any of the available "best" options. The perfect answer—a permanent structure—was something we just could not afford right now, and upon that realization I was receptive to other ideas. Faith suggested a canopy top she found in an ad as a temporary fix. While it was unable to withstand high winds or a downpour, it provided enough protection from the sun and light rains until we could afford something better.

Eventually, a permanent roof was constructed, and the carpenter was a talented man who plied his trade all over the world. Married to Faith's best friend from nursing school, John had spent several years in Africa building homes for those less fortunate as a volunteer. He met with us early in the summer to learn exactly what we envisioned, but would not be able to start construction until September. Fortunately, it had been one of the driest summers on record here in New York.

The dog days of August behind us, construction commenced each Saturday morning until sunset. John is sincerely nice, a tireless worker never complaining about working in the heat or rain. While the kennels were being erected, neighbors jokingly began referring to it as the dog palace.

By mid-October, John's work was complete. His craftsmanship was exceptional, and the kennel roof was exactly what I had hoped for. An Alaskan Malamute weather vane perched atop the newly shingled roof, compliments of Faith.

The next few weeks we spent adding finishing touches, capped by a flagpole bought and mounted by Faith from which an Alaska state flag waved in the breeze.

When cooler autumn weather arrived and with a permanent roof in place, Noah and Taylor began spending more time outside. While comfortable in their kennels, I still made sure they had regular house time just to roam around and hang in their crates.

I also continued to have them groomed. Especially Noah. Even with daily brushing, after a few months his coat is unmanageable, and I lack the necessary gear to really groom him properly. Sandy is unequaled when it comes to grooming Malamutes, having had plenty of practice over the years preparing for hundreds of dog shows and several successful trips to Westminster.

Noah hated baths but knew better than to try and pull rank on Sandy. Because he was easily distracted, I stepped out to visit with her dogs. One in particular I hoped to see was laid out on the floor, opening his eyes when he heard me coming. Lifting his head, he began to sniff the strange dog on my clothes. Only when I looked at Tyler up close do the similarities between him and Noah become apparent. Their facial expressions, gestures, and vocalizations were almost identical. If not for Tyler's wolf-gray color and a cape, I would have sworn it was Noah.

When Sandy is finished, Noah looked stunning. All prettied up, he was as beautiful outside as he was inside. My boy was happy to see me and let out a "woo."

It was raining when we arrive home. I wanted to keep Noah clean, and hoped to get him quickly from the car to kennel. But he had other plans, and headed straight for the mud. In less than one minute, he made a mess of his shiny coat.

Fortunately, a little mud could not dirty his beautiful heart.

"You do not own him - you are his alpha, not his master. You are his guardian and companion. He will always be there for you. Living with an Alaskan Malamute is a lifetime commitment."

The Forever Pasture

Living in a farmhouse with an eight-stall horse barn and five acres of fenced-in pasture, it was difficult to oppose Faith's desire for more animals. She began going to a nearby farmer auction held weekly. I have never been to one of these auctions myself, but from what she described, it sounded like a place where farmers send off livestock they have no use for. Typically, this means bull calves.

Raising a calf is burdensome, and farmers are not inclined to invest any more time or money in them than necessary. Viewed as a liability, bull calves are an inescapable inconvenience of building a milking herd, and few farmers are willing even to sell them off as veal at a later date. Sending bull calves off to auction is an inexpensive, easy way out of the problem. Most calves are sick upon arrival, never having received the necessary colostrum from their mothers' milk. Unable to leave sick or injured animals, Faith's kind heart compels her to action. I returned home from work to find one of these calves lying on our bathroom floor.

Hay was strewn across the tiled floor, and there was an unmistakable "barn" odor emanating from within, the upstairs bathroom of one's home being as unlikely a place as ever to find a newborn calf. The little guy was not well. Severely dehydrated and not eating, Faith tried everything she could think of to get him healthy.

It was a rough night for Faith, sleeping just outside the bathroom on the carpet. The next day was no better, and our little calf passed away that evening. He received more love in the twenty-four hours he was here than most calves receive in their entire lives. I buried him in the pasture.

Faith returned to the auction for another calf and brought home "Ranger," an unattractive Angus/Holstein cross with an uncommonly sweet disposition.

> My first memories weren't pleasant ones. From the warmth of the womb that had protected and nourished me for so many months, I was violently thrust into a cold world. I don't know how long I waited, scared and alone, before a crimson glow in the east began to light up the sky. Having not yet lived an hour, each minute seems an eternity to a newborn calf like me. A void in my stomach demands to be filled. Where is Mama? She must return quickly. Without knowing how to live, I will surely die.
>
> I hear the sound of approaching footsteps and then the tall grass parts. The

creature before me stands upright on shiny yellow hooves. I am picked up and carried away, the entire time my mouth searching futilely for anything that might satisfy my growing hunger. The creature eventually places me in a long shelter sitting atop black disks. It is walled in on all sides but one. I moo, "Please sir, take me back to the field so Mama can find me when she returns." The shelter darkens as a final wall is pulled down, and once again I feel the sensation of movement.

Bright light hurts my eyes when the wall is raised, and I am lifted out of my confine. I feel my hooves on the ground for the first time. It is good to be standing, but my legs are wobbly and weak. My front right leg is sore, and I am unable to put much weight on it. I am so hungry. I want only to lie back down in the field and wait for Mama. The two-legged creature with yellow hooves is shouting at me, and I am scared. I run quickly on my untested legs down a one-way path that opens up into another shelter. This place is much larger and is lit with artificial suns. It is filled with other calves just like me, and they are all scared. I am afraid, too. There are many more of these two-legged creatures, and all of them are shouting. They are bidding on us. Where is Mama?

She has long brown hair and blue eyes. Her voice is soothing and touch is gentle.

She places me in the front seat of her truck, and we go for a ride. I am then carried out to a red barn and lain down in a bed of cedar and hay. Mama sits down beside me holding a plastic bottle with a nipple made to fit my mouth. I eagerly suck and soon can feel the warm milk filling my empty stomach. When I am finished, Mama lies down next to me, and for the first time in my life I feel safe, warm, and full. I am content.

It is still early in the year, and nights can be chilly for young calves like me. I can see my breath in the air. Mama picks me up and carries me into another shelter, colored gray with a brick front. This barn must be where she lives. Together we lay down, and Mama pulls a blanket over us. The warmth of Mama's body and the beat of her heart are intoxicating. Soon, I am asleep beside her.

In the morning, after my bottle, Mama takes me for a ride. We go to a place called Pumpkin Hill, and I meet a kind man named Doctor Mathes who listens to my heart and breathing. I am poked and prodded, and he examines my front right leg. I feel a quick prick on my neck. Mama is handed a bottle of pills and is instructed to give me two each evening for the next fifteen days. These things taste awful, but she is careful to make sure I swallow each one and not spit them out.

Mama is there each morning and evening with my bottle. She has also started feeding me some kind of molasses-coated corn and grain mixture. She puts it in my mouth piece by piece. I spit some out at first, but when I see how happy it makes her watching me eat, I chew and swallow. She names me Ranger. During the day, Mama puts me out to the pasture. I love lying in the tall grass with her by my side, soaking in the warmth of the sun. Evenings are still cold. Mama tucks me in each night with a wool blanket. There are a few nights when she is worried it may be too cold for me and beds down next to me in the hay.

One day Mama introduces me to a goat named Chase. He is also young, but that is where our similarities end. While I am satisfied after my bottle, Chase is still hungry. His mouth never stops. There isn't a flower left near our barn. We are different but Chase is good company. He follows me out to the pasture every morning. While I lay in the sun next to Mama, I can see Chase's head bob up and down in the tall grass as he runs. My little goat friend is never far from me. Evenings we spend together and sleep side by side. Chase is on top of the blanket, and I am tucked underneath. The warmth of his little body pressed against mine during these cold nights is a comfort. He is my best friend.

I am never lonely for my red barn is full of friends, and Mama is always coming and going. She calls me her "kissing sponge." In addition to Chase, there are also six chickens whose company I enjoy. Early in the morning they forage in and around the barn for food. Afternoons they occasionally race around the barn floor. Most of the time they are content just to perch above my stall. When the sun goes down, one or two of them will sometimes crawl between my hooves to sleep.

Mama doesn't give me a pill tonight. I finish my bottle, she hand feeds me my oats as usual, and says I am finished having to take the pills. She lays with me in the soft hay and talks to me. I am happy here.

I wake up stiff, and my leg hurts again. I can tell Mama is concerned. She takes me for a ride, and I find myself once more at Doctor Mathes's office. He gives Mamma a bottle of medicine and needles. I am to have shots twice a day in my neck.

It's been over a week, and my medicine doesn't seem to be helping. Chase wants to go out to the pasture and play, but my leg hurts me too badly. I cannot even get up. He jumps all around me and then runs a few feet out. He looks over his shoulder to see if I've followed. Eventually, Chase gives up trying and goes off on his own.

My stomach tells me it must be near feeding time. I can hear Mama enter the barn. I try to get up and greet her but my leg buckles beneath me. My leg is sore tonight, and it is painful even to move, let alone stand. Mama looks so sad. She holds me in her arms for what feels like forever.

The morning is rainy and miserable. My back legs are sore now too. Are they stiff because of the weather? I am unable to stand and end up defecating all over myself. Mama brings out my bottle and starts to cry when she sees me. She cleans and then feeds me. Holding me close, she promises everything will be all right, and by the end of the day I will no longer be in pain. Mama returns to the house.

It hasn't been more than ten minutes and Mama is back again to see me. I can hear the rain falling outside as we lay together in the hay. Doctor Mathes stops by to visit and he is all wet. The rain is coming down harder. I feel the familiar prick of a needle. Mama hugs me once more and tells me she loves me. She gently leads me into the warm sun and tall grass—my Forever Pasture.

I buried Ranger that afternoon in our pasture. Rhythmically moving sod with a shovel, I tried making sense of it all while digging. The lives of our first two calves were valued considerably less by society than my Malamutes—the significant difference being Noah and Taylor came from a reputable breeder. Their chances for a long, healthy life were high because that breeder invested large amounts of time and money into their well-being. Their breeding was planned and took place between two finished champions.

Why is that little "Ch" In front of a dog's name so important? The conformational title of champion is earned only after several qualified persons recognize the dog as an excellent example of the breed. Alaskan Malamutes can be disqualified from earning this title for any number of reasons, including functional (poor movement, coat, etc.), aesthetic (light-colored or blue eyes), and temperamental (aggression).

Once medical clearances are complete (hips tested good or better against dysplasia, chondrodysplasia, eyes, etc.), the breeder sought a suitable mate for her bitch. "Suitable" meaning a stud that is also finished, medically tested, and offers the same high-quality characteristics.

It was determined she was certainly up to the task. Four year-old *Ch. Moon Song's Never Say Never ROM* had few if any conformational faults. The radiograph was reviewed and OFA consensus was no recognizable evidence of hip dysplasia. Her hip joint conformation was evaluated as "good." Both her and her parents were certified "clear" of hip dysplasia and declared free of chondrodysplasia. Her eyes were examined and cleared CERF# AM-553/95-27. Maija was a sweet bitch with a wonderful temperament and was going to be bred.

The same criteria had been applied when choosing her mate—*BIS BISS Am/Can Ch. Nanuke's Take No Prisoners ROM* excelled in the ring and his conformational results were outstanding. Tyler's OFA results were "excellent," and he too was certified free and clear of chondrodysplasia and hip dysplasia. Every Alaskan Malamute breeding should be as carefully planned as this one.

Maija had been restless all morning. Within the confines of the whelping box her breathing was labored as she stopped to pant after each push.

::breathe:: ::push:: ::breathe:: ::push::

Straining on that last push, a small wet bundle slid out from between her legs onto a towel. She licked the newborn and nibbled away at the placenta. A tiny black-and-white bitch named Erika was safe in her mother's care. Maija had just finished cleaning what was to be her first of seven puppies when she began to strain and push again. A seal-and-white male called Noah was next to make his way into the world, followed by Solo, Wookie, Maxwell, Hendricks, and finally Cheech.

It had been a long day and Maija was exhausted. She lay in the well-populated whelping box, nursing her new arrivals. Puppies can neither see nor hear when they are born and for the next eight weeks are completely dependent upon their mother for survival.

Maija works hard ensuring her puppies are fed, kept warm, and properly socialized. Like all good mothers, she has done her part. Eventually, she entrusts the welfare of her puppies to humans and the rest is up to us.

"Love my dog. Do not ever abuse or mistreat him. Care for the life of my dog as you would care for your own. Feed him. Groom him. Exercise him. Play with him. Teach him. Give him a soft, dry place to sleep. Walk him daily, even in the sleet and snow he will have to potty. Aid him when he is in need. Take him to the vet if ever he is injured or sick. Our body and spirit are bred for the cold Northern lands. Protect him from the heat. Keep him safe from the busy traffic and petty demands of civilization. It may sound like a lot of work, but it is no less than what I have already done.

"You do not own him—you are his alpha, not his master. You are his guardian and companion. Living with an Alaskan Malamute is a lifetime commitment. He will always be there for you. Do not forsake him. He is never to be abandoned or euthanized out of convenience. A painful day will eventually come when he is called back North to join those who have gone before him. You will ensure his departure is dignified and without suffering. My puppies are precious." - Maija.

Losing two calves so soon after being purchased at auction, neither of us could withstand more heartbreak. We needed to find a farmer that bred cows like a reputable dog breeder. Faith did her homework and contacted a woman who bred, raised, and showed Jerseys and Holsteins.

Robin took great pride in her farm. It was home to several hundred cattle, and it was immediately apparent she cared about her animals. There was food down and fresh water available. The place was clean with no evidence of animals sleeping in filth. The cows were friendly, and the experience was more akin to that of a petting zoo than a dairy farm.

Faith explained the problems we encountered with the calves she picked up at auction and our desire for one starting life out healthy. Robin assured us that all her calves were in fine fettle. So certain she was of this, she guaranteed them. Leading us over to several Jersey bull calves, she told us to pick one. Each calf had a name (as opposed to a number). Faith wrapped her arms around several, eventually settling on Clarence James.

CJ was far livelier than either of our previous calves, and the health difference was immediately obvious when Faith went to feed him. He did not suck his bottle, but attacked it. I took time to reflect on all the changes taking place in my life:

> Thirty-eight years of preparation allow me to accept continual metamorphosis, but nothing could have prepared me for this. A year ago, Noah and I resided in a one-bedroom apartment. The two of us woke up next to each other, ate, played and ran together. I lived side by side with my sole and constant companion.

Ten months and sixty miles ago, we left the little apartment behind. Noah spends the majority of his nights now sleeping next to Taylor, and it is my human companion, Faith, that I share my bed with. She is a tireless worker whose beauty is evident both inside and out. I had only known to dream and wish before Faith taught me to pursue and have. She has shown me how to hunt my dreams on the plains of reality.

Our lifestyle requires considerable work to maintain. Others question why we choose to live the way we do. Those needing to ask probably are not capable of understanding the answer.

I am grateful for the many changes that have taken place, and with a great sigh of relief, thankful for those wonderful things that have remained the same. Winter snows and long celestial nights. Polaris my guide and Northern Lights. And Noah, my beautiful seal and white.

Certainly, while many things changed this first year Faith and I lived together, all that was important to me stayed the same. The alterations were wonderful additions to the beautiful life I was already living. We continued to grow together and explore all we shared. Soaked in summer rain, we stood under rainbows that arched over acres of pasture. We wandered through woods and dirtied our feet in pumpkin patches. Celebrating each day together, we found happiness with all the animals whose lives intertwined with ours.

The warm summer gave way to a brilliant autumn display. Red and golden remnants of longer days fell to the ground and browned before color was obliterated completely by heavy snows. Winter descended, and I was spending much of it adventuring with Noah and Taylor. Never having tolerated the cold well, Faith remains inside. Change continues taking place, not all of it pleasant.

"All animals entrusted to our care, whether domestic or wild, deserve to live their lives with dignity and our compassion."

Rhythm of Compassion

The temperature fell even faster than the snow, and we lost our first chicken in January. Shirley froze to death in the coop. Faith discovered her slumped over in the nesting box, still on top of her egg. There was no hiding from the brutal west wind that afternoon.

We immediately set to work moving our chickens into the barn. An empty stall would protect them from wind, and a heat lamp hung above the perch provided extra warmth. Not a single peep was heard when we added extra cracked corn to their diet.

> It is difficult for me to empathize with those that suffer from the cold. A creature's inability to handle freezing weather never occurred to me before Shirley's loss. The ones with whom I am closest will never know what it is like to be cold.
>
> I had chicken for dinner last night (store-bought; our chickens are layers and not meant for eating) and didn't give it much

thought.   Shirley's death bothers me, though, and maybe I understand why. When we kill, we control the cessation of life. It is when Death takes a creature—the uncontrollable cessation of life—that we feel cheated.

In the spring, we will pick up a few more chicks.   We'll continue to offer our barns, land, money, and time to provide as best a home as we can to our animals.

Ultimately, Death takes all in the end. That's not to say we can't try and cheat him for a little while.

She was "mom" to one. Another trusted her as a loving wife and companion. Most others knew her as "Rose." My brother, sister, and I, we just called her "Grandma."

This winter was turning out to be a rough one. A few weeks after Shirley's death, I received a message that my grandmother had passed away. She had not been doing well. Taken ill on Christmas Eve, she was rushed to the hospital and diagnosed with congestive heart failure. I had been told at the time it was serious, and when she was moved from the hospital to hospice, I knew she would be gone soon. I was concerned for my grandfather.   Their marriage, a close and loving relationship, spanned over seventy years.   How my grandfather would react and adapt without my grandmother by his side, I would soon find out.

Taking a few days off from work, I drove to Lyons, NY, to be with my family. All of us would be together and stay with my grandfather in his home. Originally built some time in the 1880s, the house had gone through several renovations, expansions, and changes. It was converted to a duplex some time in the thirties, with an aunt of mine living on one side and my grandparents on the other. Front porches and side porches were later added in the late sixties. The original front entrance door my grandparents and father used sits at the bottom of a staircase and has been boarded up for years. It had opened up to front steps that eventually rotted and were torn out. The door looks odd just hanging there on the front of the house.

I arrived just after noon. My parents, brother, and sister were already there. "Gramps" greeted me at the door. I walked in. A pot of pasta cooking on the stove and my grandmother next to it were noticeably missing. The surroundings were familiar, yet not right. An uneasy feeling was beginning to develop inside me.

Funeral parlors are too sterile an environment for mourning. Conversation was forced as our family members tried to comfort one another. Accepting the fact grandma is gone, panic erupts nonetheless as I confront her lifeless body laid out before me. It was time to leave.

I grieve differently than most. Finding solace in the company of my pack mates, we journeyed that night under a clear sky. The Northeast was under a wicked cold spell, and it was a frigid walk under the stars. Wearing just a little less than usual for such extreme weather, my thoughts were consumed with getting warm and nothing else. Eventually we returned home and I climbed in bed next to Faith.

Winter would not relent, and it remained bitterly

cold. Even as life passed away, snow continued to fall. Warm memories of grandma haunted me while temperatures slipped below zero and arcane ice patterns were etched upon the windows. Waking up, I looked at the thermometer on the other side of the glass pane, and it reads −14° F. I feed Noah and Taylor. I quickly dressed while they eat, but my wool and down was no match in either beauty or functionality to their fur coats. The three of us headed outside.

Mornings were dull and gray since Grandma's passing. I closed my eyes and begin to run, looking only occasionally at the path in front of me, letting the Malamutes guide. A few hundred yards later, they abruptly stopped. Opening my eyes, I witnessed a most beautiful thing: as the sun rises in the East, a prismatic arch reaches over the top to create a halo with bright sun dogs positioned on each side and one above the burning sphere. Even more amazing is the arc over it all curving *away* from the halo like a prismatic smile. This upside-down rainbow is a circumzenithal arc, a rare optic phenomena caused by refracted sunlight passing through ice crystals oriented at a specific angle. That morning, as sun dogs flanked Sol and traveled across the sky, I ran with two of my own. Happiness was beginning to find its way back into my life.

Faith's boundless compassion precipitated the rescue of any animal that is sick, injured, or unable to care for itself. Many times I have come home and discovered a Canadian goose or duck unfortunate enough to wander into traffic mending in the bathtub. Abandoned cats and dogs all seem to find their way to our house. We once broke open a bag of pine shavings and uncovered two litters of mice that had just been born inside. Faith fed them with an eyedropper for several weeks. Not all survived, but those that did were released when we were confident they could fend for themselves.

Our most memorable rescue began with a stray feral cat hanging around the barn. She spent most nights sleeping in a hay stall and we left food out for her during the winter. Noah and Taylor paid little attention to this interloper after a few of her visits. We named her Caroline. When spring arrived, she gave birth to a litter of kittens between the walls of our shed. Unfortunately, she then had a hard time getting back into the four-inch space to nurse them. Upon hearing faint meows while walking past the structure, I put my ear up against the outside wall hoping it was not just my imagination. Sure enough, I could make out their high-pitched cries for Mom.

Returning to the house, I let Faith know of my discovery before retrieving a hammer and crowbar from the garage. Dismantling the interior wall of the dilapidated shed was easy work. My only concern was for the safety of the kittens as I began to pry the inside sheet of plywood from the studs. Once the job was done, we scooped up five day-old tiger-striped kittens and placed them safely into the confines of a shoebox. This allowed Faith time to set up a small shelter for them in the shed consisting of a pet carrier with a blanket stuffed inside.

We gently placed each of the kittens into the carrier and left food and fresh water for Caroline. Our hope was that she would raise the kittens there so we could try to find them homes when they got a little older. We want to avoid un-spayed and un-neutered cats from populating our land with even more litters.

But "Mom" had other plans.

From the house, we watched Caroline return to the shed—and leave again just a few minutes later. In the course of twenty minutes, we watched her go in and out of the shed four times. Her behavior seemed odd, so we checked on the kittens. There was only one kitten left inside the pet carrier. Instead of raising her kittens there, she was moving them out. We searched the property to no avail.

We took the lone kitten inside and christened him Little Joe Cartwright. To prevent any of the Malamutes from using him as a chew toy, he was kept in the bathroom with the door closed at all times until we could figure out other arrangements. Faith made a cozy bed for him inside a birdcage and placed that in our empty bathtub so Little Joe could wander out and yet not get into trouble. I picked up supplies for his care, including formula and a small bottle.

Every morning Little Joe cried to let us know he is up and hungry. Faith mixed formula into a bottle with warm water and fed him. Unfortunately, Little Joe awoke earlier each day. On Saturday morning, after we had worked all week, we could hear the cries. I opened my eyes, and the room was still dark. Thrusting a finger into my Faith's side, she groans. "I know. I can hear him. What time is it?"

"Three fifty-five."

Faith rose and slowly made her way to the bathroom. A few minutes later she returned to bed. The crying had stopped.

"Did you feed him or kill him?!"

"He's fine. He can eat when we get up today."

Faith had brought the birdcage containing Little Joe outside and placed it in the car.

A few weeks later we stumbled across two more of Little Joe's siblings in the barn and were able to corner each of them in a stall. I brought out one of the extra dog crates to put them in until we figured out what to do. Now we just needed to get them from the stall into the crate. The task required a fishing net and heavy leather gloves. The first one caught was a frightened longhair female. Her brother, a blond tiger stripe, was next and full of fury. I figured he might simmer down once he was reunited with his sister. But, with fire in his eyes, he clung to the side of the crate, hissing and spitting.

Neither of us believed that either cat could be tamed. The plan was to keep them in the garage until they were old enough to be spayed and neutered, and then release them. Benny "Boo" and "Crazy" Daisy Mae both hid in the far corner of the garage for several weeks.

Benny was the first to come around. One morning while getting breakfast ready for the dogs, he walked up within arm's reach and sat in front of me. Tilting his head to the side, he stared at me with bright green eyes, almost as if waiting for me to do something. I slowly brought my hand around so he could give it a sniff. Unlike a dog, Benny had little interest in sniffing my hand, and instead began rubbing against it. This went on for several days until one morning I scooped him up into my arms. Scratching behind his ears elicited a loud purr. Benny was "domesticating." Soon after, Daisy Mae came around as well.

When the time came to reunite Benny and Daisy with their brother, both cats were ambivalent to Little Joe's arrival. Little Joe, however, sat on the concrete floor, shaking uncontrollably. I left the garage but continued listening for trouble. A few hours later, Little Joe is still sitting there with his face to the door. The next morning, though, Little Joe is curled up in a cat bed with Benny and Daisy, settling in nicely with his brother and sister.

We eventually found out that a fourth kitten was living in a neighbor's barn and had made a nice home for herself there.

One kitten of the litter was still unaccounted for, however, and it was on a rainy night in October when we came across a small tiger-striped female sitting on the side of the road. Exiting the car, I scooped her up from the pavement. She was soaking wet and thin, and we brought her home. Minnie Pearl lived happily with her siblings ever since—and all of them were spayed, neutered, cared for and loved.

I had learned how to properly care for Noah and Taylor and discovered that those lessons are not exclusive to Alaskan Malamutes. It is quite simple, really—all animals entrusted to our care, whether domestic or wild, deserve to live their lives with their dignity and our compassion.

"Physical activity and mental stimulation are essential for an Alaskan Malamute. Just like their human counterparts, it is the idle Malamute that gets into trouble."

Diamonds and Rust

Alaskan Malamutes are an active breed. Their natural talents, combined with an efficient metabolism and high energy level, allow them to excel in cold environments. Bred to pull heavy sleds, they thoroughly enjoy strenuous activity. This was evident by the excitement Noah and Taylor exuded when they saw me with their harnesses. Similarly, because of their ancient ability to navigate endless fields of snow and ice, Malamutes are often used for search and rescue. Physical activity and mental stimulation are essential for their well-being. Just like humans, the idle Malamute gets into trouble.

Northern Lights mirror my quest.
The dogs are tired but we'll not rest.
North Star will guide us till morning's sun.
I mush to live, and they live to run.

Wearing out Noah was physically challenging. We ran several miles each morning. Taylor's workouts were not as taxing, and being older, she was content with a long walk. Whenever they were left unattended for any length of time, it is always after physical activity. Even then, both were settled in their crates, chewing on bones in front of the television before I leave.

While I was busy at work, Noah recharged his batteries, anxiously awaiting my return. Walking through the door, even after a long day, I no longer bothered taking off my coat. Unlatching each crate liberated the furred dynamite contained within. Rushing past me as if released from under pressure, both Malamutes met me at the door. Heads quickly slipped into collars and we went out for a romp.

Exercise and mental stimulation are important but neither replaces the need for human interaction. Alaskan Malamutes are not content as an accessory to one's life; they demand to be an active part of it. Noah and Taylor wanted to be where I was, and do what I am doing.

We were not in our house more than a few months when Faith was laid off, a fate common to many during the economic downturn. Unemployment benefits helped cover bills while she searched for work as a software tester, but the entire tech industry continued tightening its belt by shedding employees.

A year later, still unable to find work in her profession, Faith took whatever available jobs she could, first as a home health aide and then in a law firm. She eventually enrolled in nursing school and became a registered nurse. Her intelligence and compassion lend themselves well to this occupation. Faith lined up work in the surgical unit at a local hospital and would never again have trouble finding work.

School is the equivalent of a full-time job, only one does not get paid to attend. We had been surviving on one income for two years, and while the bills were paid, we lived on a tight budget and never afforded ourselves much in the way of luxury. Our monthly income now more than doubled, Faith treated herself to something she has always wanted—a metal detector.

Anxious to begin searching for buried treasure, I quickly assembled her new toy. Batteries not included, the smoke alarm was raided for it's 9-volt power cell. Faith was soon out the door looking for rare coins and diamond rings.

Hours later she returned home with her grandiose dreams of wealth on hold. Filthy hands clenched her recent find: rusty nails, a few corroded bolts, and a bottle cap. Discerning what might be worth the trouble to dig up yet to be mastered, she thrust her frustration into my hands. "You try."

Walking up and down the road with the metal detector swinging like a pendulum, I set out looking for riches. My first attempt with the gadget yielded more of the same junk. Similar to wandering with Noah and Taylor, the metal detector is not nearly as fun. The difference being with them, instead of looking for something interesting, I am actually doing something interesting.

Malamutes are also detectors of sorts. With their noses close to the ground, they too are searching for something. While Noah was unable to distinguish between ferrous and non-ferrous, the metal detector has yet to signal the foul odor of road kill or deer poop.

"Malamutes do not harbor grudges and have a huge capacity for forgiveness. There is much we humans can learn from our canine companions. Noah can forgive me for being human. I suppose it is the least I can do for others sharing the same fault."

Heart of a Malamute

Communication is key to establishing a rewarding relationship with any creature. Meaningful connections require not only sending messages, but ensuring that information is received and understood as well. Breakdowns occur when people attempt to communicate with animals as if they were human. Dogs are unable to comprehend their human companions in these instances, as we are literally talking to them in a foreign language. Compounding this breakdown is the fact that few humans ever take the time to understand what their dog is trying to communicate to *them.*

Noah can understand and communicate only like an Alaskan Malamute. If I am to effectively communicate with him, then I must to learn to speak *and* listen— like an Alaskan Malamute. Listening is a big part of the communication process between human and dog, as there were times Noah needed to convey important information to me.

One very important statement needs to be made early and that is establishing who is "alpha." Malamutes are pack animals (just like their brethren, the wolves) and demand leadership. When their human companion is unwilling (or unable) to take on that role, then the Malamute will and problems quickly arise. Much has been written already about pack structure and establishing hierarchy.* My own experience in establishing and maintaining the alpha position are as follows:

I control the food. I decide where and when it is time to eat. I eat first and do so in front of them. I control entry and exit to all locations, both in the house and at the kennels, by either physical occupation or through the use of gates and doors. I proceed through all narrow openings first including the doorway. I restrict movement of all lesser-ranked by the use of collars, leads, and fencing. Only I am allowed unlimited access to "prime spots" within the house such as on the bed or in front of a door. I do not walk around pack mates; I insist they move to let me pass. Activities I wish to discourage are met with an icy glare, firm command, and then baring my teeth. (A big toothy smile works best.)

Dog aggression many times boils down to a dominance issue. Noah understood that biting is wrong, but occasionally he tested limits and issued a challenge. When that occurred, I immediately asserted myself as "alpha." Hoping to quickly clear up any misunderstanding over who calls the shots, I found that sometimes the only way to accomplish this was to grab his muzzle, roll him over on his back, look him straight in the eye, and yell. Fear of death was enough to elicit submission, not the actual act of dying itself. The threat alone that undesirable behavior can abruptly cause life to end was key. There is never a need to strike or beat a dog. Not under *any* circumstance. Inflicting pain does not establish dominance; it only fuels resentment. While Alaskan Malamutes have an incredibly high tolerance for pain, striking one is abuse that can injure them physically and destroy them emotionally.

Once submission has been demonstrated, it is important to immediately back off. This is how dominance is communicated among canines, and to ensure no misunderstanding, it is vital to communicate on their terms.

Noah's apology went like this: When he whimpered and yielded, I stopped yelling and got off of him. When I let him up, he was a completely different dog, putting his paws on my shoulders and showering me with kisses. All was forgiven, and we were best friends again.

Arguing with Noah was never enjoyable and could be downright dangerous. I picked and chose our battles, especially with dominance-related issues. Sometimes a physical altercation was unavoidable. When a situation had potential to cause him great harm, sometimes it became necessary to physically force my will upon his. One particular incident, in which some kid decided that the lunch his mom packed was not worth bringing to school and tossed the peanut butter sandwich (still in plastic wrap) to the ground, led to a tussle. There were others as well.

Heavy snowfall during February is typical for western New York, and the drive between Rochester and Buffalo can be treacherous. What should have been an hour-long ride home from helping a friend was now closer to two. The sore throat and stuffy nose I woke up with that morning had developed into a full-blown cold by the time I finally pulled into the driveway.

Overtired and feverish, all that was required of me before bed was letting the dogs out to go potty. Noah came storming out of his crate. Standing in front of the sliding glass patio door with the lead in my hand, his head slipped through the collar. I opened the door and walked out with him into the cold. Snow was falling like confetti coming down at a ticker tape parade, and the wind was drifting toward a heavy accumulation. It was the kind of night we lived for. I had no desire to trek through the blizzard though and only wanted to climb into bed. "They're all good spots," I told Noah. "Pick one and go potty."

The heavy sliding door is usually problematic when it freezes and never pulls completely shut. While holding the lead in my left hand, I stuck my right hand behind me and gave the door a good tug to close it the rest of the way. Maybe it was ice in the track or my own fever-induced inattentiveness, but the glass door flew closed as if the track had been greased. My hand smashed hard against the house, and two seconds later a severe wave of pain followed the impact. Letting go of the lead, I looked at the injury and concluded that my finger was broken.

Noah should have just found a spot to go potty but inches of fresh snow snapped the reality circuit in his brain and had him thinking we somehow magically transported to somewhere along the Kotzebue Sound. His adventure level shot from zero to one hundred. Ripping around in circles, he was looking to be attached to some non-existent sled's gangline. Inadvertently catching his back paw in the lead's hand loop brought him back to reality. Firmly entangled, he turned to see what was gripping his back paw as the lead pulled tight on the collar around his neck. Going ballistic, he snapped his jaws at the invisible foe persecuting him. I moved to free him up, hoping I could simply undo the lead from his collar. Noah must have felt a primitive satisfaction as his jaws locked upon a limb of his unseen adversary. For the second time in less than a minute, I prepared myself for the great pain that would surely follow this bite.

I stood over him with my forearm in his jaws as the snow swirled around us. "Butt down!"

Noah sat on the ground before realizing it was my arm between his jaws and not that of his invisible tormentor. "May I have it back?" I politely growled.

He met my gaze and slowly released his grip, raising his right paw to shake. I ignored the gesture of goodwill and assessed the damage to my arm. While he tagged me good, I was fortunate that my sweatshirt took most of the ripping. Skin was broken in several places but there were no deep puncture wounds, just crushed tissue. It was going to leave a large bruise. My finger did not fare as well. Definitely fractured, it was swollen and beginning to throb.

Noah lowered his right paw and raised the left. I accepted the apology and shook his paw to let him know that this "misunderstanding" was behind us: "That was my *arm*, goofball, not your lead."

He gave me a quick lick on the nose and then finally settled on a spot to go potty.

A beautiful heart, one free of pettiness, deceit, and malevolence—that is the heart of a Malamute. They do not harbor grudges and have a huge capacity for forgiveness. There is much we humans can learn from our canine companions. Noah can forgive me for being human. I suppose it is the least I can do for others sharing the same fault.

*Those desiring to learn more are encouraged to invest in a copy of *Leader of the Pack*, by Nancy Baer and Steve Duno (Harper Paperbacks).

"I've heard it said a dog is man's best friend and agree. It is sad that man is unable to be man's best friend. Maybe one day he can be if we learn to love each other unconditionally, like dogs love us. Maybe one day when we are able to put the needs of those we profess to love before our own."

The Nexus of Love

Our telephone seems to ring louder once the sun goes down. A woman on the other end introduced herself as our local dog warden. Naturally, I immediately thought something was wrong with Noah and Taylor. Her reason for calling had nothing to do with my own dogs, but with two Siberian Huskies recently picked up. They had belonged to a young couple in town. During a domestic dispute, police were called to try and settle things down. A fire recently destroyed their home and neither of them wanted anything to do with the dogs, so the warden was desperate to find them homes. Having driven by our place numerous times, she was familiar with our setup and thought we might be interested in adopting them —or at least fostering until she could find a suitable placement. I agreed to meet with her the next day to take a look at the Sibes.

She was waiting in her truck when I arrived at the pound and told me all she knew about "Prince" and "Princess," who were sixteen-month-old litter mates. Prince was not neutered and Princess was not spayed; in fact, she'd given birth to a sole pup just a few months earlier. Neither dog had ever been inside, and both craved the companionship of humans.

I was led into the pound, and both dogs were there to greet me. Prince, a black-and-white with blue eyes, immediately showered me with kisses. Princess, white with one eye blue and the other brown, cautiously approached and sniffed. It was immediately evident that their previous alleged family had spent little time with either of them, and both squealed with delight to have a visitor. It seemed that one's capacity for happiness depends largely on how much one has suffered.

With both dogs loose in the enclosed area, I worked out a game plan with the warden. I agreed to temporarily foster both dogs if she was unable to find them a permanent home in the next week. Quickly snapping a few pictures to show Faith, I began formulating how to present this to her.

Enjoying the few minutes of freedom they got each day, neither Sibe wanted to return to the kennel. With considerable effort, we got both inside and the doors secured. As I went home to care for my own dogs, I thought of how a dog is a living creature with feelings, each having needs to be met and love to give.

I fail to understand how people can cast aside their canine companions. A baffling case of abandonment had already resulted in our adoption of a shepherd/beagle mix. Faith's aunt has a home two hours south of our own, and her neighbor is pastor of the local church. The pastor decided one day that he, his wife, and their children were moving. They posted a sign in their yard: "Free Dog." They were willing to leave behind something of incredible value—the loyalty, trust, and companionship of Brandy. Faith was in tears after hearing of this and immediately made arrangements for Brandy to live with us. The pastor's actions were incomprehensible to me. God places some fool in a position to oversee the "flock," but this guy could not even keep a commitment to care for his dog.

I care little for religion. Man has always perceived himself more important than any other creature, and thumbing through a Bible, it is evident that this God favors his least impressive creation over animals as well. That is not the god for me. Noah has taught me that all life is to be revered.

The reasons that owners choose to abandon their dogs are varied, yet each sounds like a ridiculous excuse. To visualize just how foolish these justifications are, substitute "dog" with "child" and "puppy" with " baby." Suppose someone is instead dropping off their child. How legitimate do these reasons look now?

1. "I didn't realize how expensive a child is."
2. "My child peed all over the rug."
3. "This child is vicious with a history of biting."
4. "I can't get any sleep. My baby whines all night long."
5. "My husband got a new job out of state, and we're relocating into a smaller place. We won't have enough room for a

child."

6. "He's a good-looking child, I'm sure he'll find another home."
7. "I can't get a moment's peace. All my child wants to do is play."
8. "My child refuses to take a bath."
9. "After careful reconsideration, I decided that I'm really not ready for a child after all."
10. "My husband passed away and I never really wanted this child to begin with."
11. "My child tracks dirt into the house."
12. "This isn't an 'outdoor' child. He's always making noise at the window to be inside with me."
13. "My new girlfriend doesn't like children."
14. "My child digs holes in the backyard."
15. "My child won't stay off the sofa."
16. "We are redecorating, and my child doesn't match the furniture."
17. "We are going on vacation and don't want to bring a baby along."
18. "My child doesn't get along with our dog."
19. "He's not as cute as when he was younger."
20. "My child is too difficult to potty-train."
21. "My child requires too much care. I just don't have enough time anymore."
22. "My child has become too destructive."
23. "I can never find a sitter for my child."
24. "My child isn't the right color."

Just as bad as the abandonment of a dog is the unwillingness of a person to care for one. Dogs are living creatures just like people and have the same basic needs—food, fresh water, health care, and companionship. An audible sign of neglect is continual barking.

When I am out I hear dogs bark.
::woof:: ::woof:: ::woof:: ::woof::
They bark constantly and at all hours.
::woof:: ::woof:: ::woof:: ::woof::
Does anyone listen to what they're saying?
They're trying to tell you something.
They're trying to tell you they're hungry and they need to be fed. They're thirsty and they need to drink water. If you can't take care of your dog's basic needs, consider planting a tree instead.
::woof:: ::woof:: ::woof:: ::woof::
They're trying to tell you that they're hot. They cannot survive outside chained to a pole when it's 90 degrees and sunny or locked in a car with the windows rolled up. If you're going to leave your dog stuck somewhere, consider just getting a picture of one and hang it on your wall instead.
::woof:: ::woof:: ::woof:: ::woof::
They're trying to tell you they're bored. They need challenges that stimulate both mentally and physically. They desire to run and play and jump and chase. If you can't

find the necessary time to spend with your dog, consider a stuffed animal instead.
::woof:: ::woof:: ::woof:: ::woof::
They're trying to tell you they love you. They want to be with you. They need your attention and affection. If you can't make your dog part of your life, then don't consider a dog at all.

I never heard back about fostering the Sibes, and believe that Prince and Princess were adopted into wonderful homes, hopefully even together.

Many say Noah was lucky. He was well-cared for, fed, had a soft place to sleep at night, and received abundant attention. Compared to those Sibes, he was certainly better off, but I would not call him lucky. He got exactly what he deserved. I am the lucky one, fortunate for the opportunity to share my life with an Alaskan Malamute.

It has been said a dog is man's best friend, and I agree. Truly sad though is the fact that *man* is unable to be man's best friend. Maybe one day he can be—if we learn to love each other unconditionally, like dogs love us. Maybe one day when we are able to put the needs of those we profess to love before our own.

"Compelled to serenade the night, her untroubled haunting cries reverberated through the blackness."

Shadow's Song

Sharper than the waning crescent moon that was just beginning to rise, her howl pierced through the darkness.

"Faith, do you hear it?"

Groggily: "Yeah, what is it?"

"That's Shadow. She's singing."

The Malamute let out another long, drawn-out howl, and my wife sat up in bed.

"It's beautiful!"

Compelled to serenade the night, her untroubled haunting cries reverberated through the blackness.

Shadow was temporarily kenneled by us late one summer while her family vacationed in Rome. I had been informed beforehand that she would occasionally regurgitate meals. She had been previously examined for this but the cause remained unknown. Otherwise, she appeared healthy. A big girl, she stood taller than Noah with color and markings similar to Taylor's. Yellow wolf-like eyes were set into chiseled gray features. Not particularly attractive by any Malamute standard, she was lovable nonetheless.

Shadow took the empty far kennel. Shy and Sandy cautioned me that introducing a third Malamute would likely cause friction in the existing order, especially between two females. Keeping that in mind, I swapped Noah and Taylor, placing him between both bitches. The arrangement did not lend itself to my anticipated outcome. Shadow's strong-willed attitude was in no way endearing to Noah while Taylor displayed complete ambivalence to this new arrival's existence. Eventually, an uneasy truce was worked out and calm restored.

Shadow was not used to being treated like an Alaskan Malamute, and I immediately established a routine of having her accompany Noah and I on morning runs. Her one idiosyncrasy was she did not like her food moistened and insisted it be served dry. She was inseparable from me until her family's return.

While glad to see her, evidently they were less than thrilled to be taking her home and expressed a few problems with neighbors who complained about the late-night howling. I shared some of my own experiences with the breed and advised just to love her like a Malamute—and made it clear that she would always have a home here if things did not work out. Faith was certain we had not heard the last of her sweet voice.

Crisp autumn days segued into long solstitial nights and then one blustery winter evening, the call came. Shadow's family needed to make changes. Wanting to place her in a loving home, they remembered my offer, and I made arrangements to take her in. Anticipating her eventual return, Noah still occupied the middle kennel.

This time the transition was much smoother, with each Malamute having already established their place in the pack order.

I immediately began taking Shadow along with us on morning runs again. She was thin but appeared to be in good shape. It is not uncommon for Malamutes to shed a few pounds during the winter, but I was concerned her weight loss was due to continually regurgitating meals. Still, she loved to eat and would attack her bowl during each feeding. I thought she would put on a few pounds by slowly changing her over to the same high-calorie diet Noah and Taylor were fed and even supplemented her food with peanut butter and fish oil, but nothing seemed to resolve the problem.

A few mornings later the kennel floor was covered with blood and bile. Shadow was uninterested in food and could not hold water down. The vet was able to see her that afternoon and performed a battery of tests. She was treated for dehydration and electrolyte imbalance. Warning she was gravely ill, the doctor emphasized she would need to be hospitalized if there was no noticeable improvement within twelve hours.

I slept little that evening checking on Shadow frequently. Scratching her belly in the darkness, I did not return to bed, waiting out the night beside her instead. Extremely lethargic at sunrise, her water had not been touched and I brought her back for hospitalization. Several hours later I went to visit, bringing along her blanket and a few stuffed toys.

The attending vet pulled me aside and explained that my new Malamute suffered from megaesophagus brought on by myasthenia gravis—in other words, her esophageal muscle contraction was impaired by a decreased functioning of the acetylcholine receptors. The smooth muscle that lined her esophagus was no longer able to move food or water into her stomach.

Her condition was irreversible; Shadow was not just starving to death but painfully dying. I contacted Faith to let her know and then go to say goodbye.

I followed the vet tech into a small pen. Always happy to see me, Shadow thought we were leaving and stood up. I kneel beside her. Anticipating what would happen next, I wrapped my arms underneath her belly. Shadow's legs went limp, and when I felt her heart stop, I lowered her body to the ground. Though we were together just a few weeks, I miss her as if it had been a lifetime. Her song, however brief to our ears, made a lasting impression on our hearts.

"Malamutes are not just expensive, but time-consuming as well. It is no longer a question of how many hours there are in a day, but rather, how much more of the day can you fit into those few hours? You don't sacrifice your time for this—give it willingly."

Arctic Dreams

Faith and I have shared our lives with many animals over the years. Some we adopted, while others were strays. Occasionally, one might just need a home for a night or two. We do our best to rehabilitate the injured and nurse the sick back to health. I have cared for numerous creatures, but none have I loved like my Alaskan Malamutes.

I have learned much from these Malamutes, Noah in particular. He taught me many things, all of which help make me a better human. What I thought our relationship would be is far different than what it became. Things I once considered important are of little value to me now, and that which I believed insignificant has taken on a whole new meaning. The journey Noah and I have taken together has proven paramount to any destination.

Life with an Alaskan Malamute, especially

on a cold winter night, is an adventure approaching the unreal. Many sit inside on such evenings by a warm fire, imagining the experience yet never knowing. People such as these are content to dream. Those who want to be must look beyond romantic notions, set aside doubts, and go about making that dream a reality—their reality.

It is expensive to care for Malamutes. Plan on a weekly bag of high-performance dog food plus monthly heartworm medication, annual booster shots and dog licenses. There are regular appointments with the vet and unexpected visits that are not so routine. Chew toys, dog treats, steel combs and the occasional bottle of Crown Royal #3 conditioner add to an already exorbitant amount of money that you find you eagerly pay.

Malamutes are not just costly, but time-consuming. Walks, long or short, take a bite out of the day. Not only does the body need exercise, but the mind as well. Scrub the kennels, change bedding, and plan on cleaning up another mess. Bathe, brush, and groom (this includes the nails too). It is no longer a question of how many hours there are in a day, but rather how much more of the day can you fit into those few hours? Time is not sacrificed for this—it is given willingly.

Up early every morning to run. Many miles you will journey together across asphalt, dirt trails, and snow-covered fields. A month later it is time for another pair of boots. Easily covering over a thousand miles a year with your dog, you burn more calories in that first morning hour than most people will burn all day. It is a physically demanding routine. Jobs are supposed to be hard work, but this? Living with a Malamute is not some necessary encumbrance you must submit to, it is a privilege you relish.

Winter descends and blankets the world in white. Breath hangs in the air. Dress warm. Through deep snow and bitter cold, this is their world.

Why would one desire a dog that does not come when called? Aren't dogs supposed to be obedient? Malamutes have selective hearing. "Heel," "sit," "down," and "stay" are suggestions best used with other breeds. You're better off with commands such as "gee," "haw," "on by," and "go." Dog hair is considered a condiment in our house, as this breed blows coat twice a year. Another hole to fill in the yard. Sure, it can get frustrating. There is no time for a fit or tantrum. Accept it. Deal with it, and move on.

These are creatures of the Arctic that will forever change one's life. They are born and bred to work and live by our side in the cold. They are demanding, predatory, and fiercely independent. There is no master, only alpha. Work and play, sleep and live as equals. There are dogs and then there are Alaskan Malamutes. Not an obligation, more than a responsibility, and greater than any other commitment—theirs is a way of life.

Shy finished school and began working as a radiological technician. Traveling around the country with Erika, she was taking contract assignments in beautiful locations like Duluth, Minnesota, Flagstaff, Arizona, and Boulder, Colorado. She stayed for a few months in each area before moving on to the next, all the while searching for that special place with a cabin where she could finally settle again. I occasionally received e-mails and a few pictures of her adventures. Her future was bright, things were going well, and she sounded happier than I ever knew her to be. On my birthday, I received the following message:

Wild,

This is the hardest email I have ever had to write. I lost Erika today. She died of a tumor that hemorrhaged in her stomach.

We had a wonderful walk this morning and even saw some prairie dogs playing, and she was amazed. When we got back home she ate and we rough housed on the bed until she got tired and wanted to sleep. After about an hour or so, she got up and laid on my lap, pawing me to pet her beautiful face. I think she knew.

It was only a few hours later that I had to say goodbye to my best friend and love of my life. I have never felt so lonely, and coming back home was awful. I am empty and heartbroken. I miss her so much.

I can't talk on the phone today, but when I feel better I will call you. Please hug Noah and Taylor for me. I was blessed to have Erika in my life.

Love,
Shy

Just like her father, Ben, Taylor has aged gracefully. Noah had noticeably slowed. I continued to run each morning, but he was no longer able to accompany me. Content to wait in his kennel, he came to prefer the brisk walk we took upon my return each day. We did not go far, as his back legs start to shake uncontrollably. The vet believed he was suffering from the canine equivalent of Parkinson's disease, but did not know for certain. Whatever the reason, I realized we could no longer do some of the things we used to. Noah would have certainly tried if allowed. He was strong-willed and clung to his pride. I was aware of his limitations and let him think our activities were cut short because I was tired. It is not a burden to care for my Malamutes as they get older. It is an honor.

Many nights while Faith worked late at the hospital, I slept with them, next to their crates. Sometimes, I helped Noah upstairs and kept him in the bedroom with me, just like we used to do years before in our apartment. He was good for several hours but eventually wanted to return and sleep next to his sister.

She could have been doing something interesting without him, you know.

The physical infirmities that accompany age are inevitable. It is called getting old. I can easily distinguish these "twilight" years from the dawn of our relationship by the passage of time. Take, for example, a sunset. The sun travels from east to west and at day's end, as it sits on the horizon, the sky is colored with a beautiful orange and crimson glow. Were one able to stop time, the sky looks almost identical to what they might have witnessed that morning, twelve or so hours earlier. Looking at the sky with no regard to direction, one is unable to determine if the sun is rising or setting. When each moment is played out together—second after second, adding up to minutes and then hours—the sun travels across the sky, and then we can distinguish that it is setting.

Only with the passage of time does one realize they are old. Living in the moment, one no longer perceives they are old, only that they are alive. Noah knew this all along. With a mind clear of what was or what will be, a Malamute is focused on what is now.

"It is our responsibility not only to help maintain a creature's dignity in life, but see to it they die with their pride intact as well."

When Northern Lights Dim

One inevitable aspect of our relationship was one we had yet to share. While I gave Noah many things, this last gift proved to be the kindest, most difficult one to bestow. His quality of life deteriorating and his dignity beginning to suffer beyond what a Malamute should bear, I knew he would be leaving me soon.

His back legs had given out completely, and for the second morning in a row Noah was unable to get up. His efforts to stand and greet me at the kennel door were in vain, and his frustration soon gave way to fear. Wrapping my arms under his back end, I hoisted him upright and, with supporting hands, he took a few steps. I cleaned him as best I could, drying both legs with a towel and removing crusted feces from his tail. We slowly walked over to the clean bedding I had brought out, and I gently lowered him onto it.

Noah had no interest in food again either, turning his nose away even from the baked chicken strips in his bowl. He licked at several of the ice cubes placed in front of him and crushed one between his teeth, but without adequate intake of water he was headed for trouble. It was then I understood that this was our last day together.

The vet agreed to see us immediately. I quickly made a bed for Noah in the back of the truck, laying his blanket over a quilted comforter, and gathered his favorite stuffed toys. Bunny, Louis the swan, and Alien will be there with him. Faith insisted on driving us and notified her work that she was taking the day off.

Galvanized metal made a distinctive clank as I unlatched the kennel door and walked over to Noah. He remained silent but expresses unmistakably:

When you can't run, you crawl. And when you can't crawl, when you can no longer do that...

"You find someone to carry you." I said, finishing his thought out loud. Carefully lifting Noah, I brought him to the truck and sat beside him, stroking his fur on this final ride.

There were few parking spaces available and none close to the entrance. I dreaded the thought of having to lift my boy again and carry him through a busy waiting area into an exam room. Hoping to spare him this unnecessary stress, I asked Faith to see if the vet would come to us instead.

Opening the back hatch and lowering the tailpiece allows me room to wrap my arms around Noah's neck. The next few minutes would be our last together. Pulling him close, I kissed the black strip on his nose. I have kissed that strip over a hundred thousand times now. Scratching the thick fur behind his ears, I looked into his brown eyes.

"I love you. You're my best friend—the most wonderful companion I could ever have. Thank you for

138

everything. You showed me how to be a better human. You taught me how to laugh and love and forgive. You taught me how to live. Now you are teaching me how to say 'goodbye.' I'll miss you. You won't be forgotten, and I'll share with everyone your memory. I treasure what we've shared."

Letting me know all is well, Noah licked my face.

The vet greeted us as she approached the truck. Explaining that it was her job to keep animals alive, she asked if I am sure this is the day. Yesterday was "the day." Last week could have been "the day."

I nodded. "Yes, I am certain today is the day."

Unable to find a vein in Noah's back leg, poor circulation forces her to dispatch a lethal dose of compassion into his front paw. Burying my face into the thick fur of Noah's neck, I whispered, "You can see a shimmering curtain starting to part—that's Erika on the other side. It's okay. Run to her, she's been waiting for you. One day you'll meet me at this very spot when my time comes to join you. We'll be together again—I promise. I'll always love you."

Noah's body went limp in my arms, our beautiful snow globe shattering as it crashed upon the ground. My tears soaked his muzzle. Placing my nose on top of his head, I inhaled deeply, knowing it would be a lifetime before I am favored with that scent again.

His spirit released, I brought Noah's body in for cremation. All that remains are his dog tags, a green lead, and some stuffed toys—small mementos left behind of a reality no one else could fully understand or see.

Returning home, Taylor anxiously paced in the kennel, waiting for her brother to jump out of the truck.

She would see him again soon, but not this day. "I miss him too," I told her. "It's just us now."

Dignity may not be necessary for life, but it is an essential ingredient to truly *live*. No dignity remains when one is unable to perform those things that define their existence. With some creatures, it may be the inability to perform such basic tasks as eating or loss of bowel/bladder control, while for others it can be something more complex.

Wild canines do not suffer their pack to tend their illness, yet euthanasia of humans continues to be a sensitive area of discussion. When our own dignity declines because of age-related failures and society becomes burdened with our care, it is an individual's inalienable right—their responsibility—to decide whether to end their life. Because our Malamute companions have entrusted us with their lives, their care is our responsibility, including any end-of-life decisions. We are tasked not only to help maintain their dignity in life, but see to it that they die with their pride intact as well.

It is never easy to see one you love failing and know that ultimately, there is only one inevitable outcome. We do what we must. While we care for and tackle seemingly impossible ailments and tasks, we cherish each moment as we see finality drawing closer. We continue to love.

It is painful to watch hips stiffen and the limp get worse or see the results of blood work indicating organs are starting to fail. It is difficult to watch the friend you love, suffer and decline in health. You do things you never would have done before, like carrying them up and down stairs or supporting them upright with your hands wrapped around their belly so they can go potty. Moistened food is often left in a bowl to be eaten at leisure. Recognizing a bad day for exactly what it is and knowing it will pass, often conditions deteriorate further before they get better.

When that fateful day arrives, you know. There is no easy way to explain it. While you were shaking your head, thinking this too is just another bad day, realization sets in. This day is one unlike any other—the day you must say goodbye.

It is never easy, even when you might see it coming. Too quickly it can transform into a nightmare of tubes, transfusions, emergency vet visits, and emotional turmoil. You will be confused. You will not feel you are thinking clearly because you are probably severely sleep-deprived. You will be rushed to make decisions you are not sure about—even though the outcome will ultimately be the same. In the end you feel a profound sense of loss. You may second-guess your decisions and torture yourself with guilt over things you did or might not have done.

Confronting things we don't necessarily want to, such situations must be faced with as much strength and courage as we can muster. In the end, it was never about us. We offer a life of health, happiness, and love, then a dignified death. That is really not such a bad thing if you think about it—being surrounded by those who love you most, holding you close, kissing your muzzle, and reassuring you that it is all right to go, knowing that one day you will meet again.

The bond between Noah and myself remains powerful. Our hearts having been locked together in a gravitational-like dance, the strength of the attractive force between us remains undiminished even in his absence. Love is the sharp teeth of a canine and long ago I placed my heart between his jaws. There is a significant difference in our life spans, and I chose to run with one I eventually would not be able to keep up with. The old adage "time heals all wounds" may be true, but our own amount of time is finite. What if there is not enough left in a life for a heart to mend?

The French philosopher René Daumal, in his unfinished final book, details an expedition up the allegorical Mount Analogue. Climbing alongside his fictional adventurers, I have learned much from my own ascent up that mountain. When faced with a painful event that no amount of time can heal, monumental loss can be overcome by rearranging Maslow's Hierarchy of Needs—depriving one's self of basic needs to suppress more advanced needs. Call it Need Deprivation Theory.

Below... It is natural to be hurt
and feel pain over the loss of a relationship.
It is true time will
eventually make the pain go away.
There are cases, however,
when not enough time remains in a life
for it to heal. In these situations
more drastic measures to heal are required.
Some needs take priority over others.
Heartache is a feeling
when the need to belong is not met.
Forcibly deprive yourself
of your more primary physical needs
and you can suppress the urge for lesser
needs.
Let your need for water go unsatisfied
and your thirst will become a
preoccupation.
As your core body temperature drops,
you fight for warmth
and your thirst is forgotten.
Above 8,000 meters
the mountain steals your breath.
When deprived of air, that extra piece of
down or Gore-Tex no longer seems
important.
Neither does the pain of a broken heart.

Life with a Malamute is magic, and Noah wove for me a beautiful tapestry of memories I will cherish always. I believe there is a reason for everything. While bothered by the frailty of life, I accept it and recognize its uniqueness.

We are surrounded by great beauty, yet life is often accompanied by the ugliness of ignorance, intolerance, and suffering. Not heartbeat and respiration, but happiness, joy, and even pain. It is these things that indicate life. The marks one can leave on a quantum fluctuation are transitory so what then is the point of living, regardless of condition? I have confidence that with life there is purpose, and of our own volition we drag meaning into existence.

A string does not pick its tension and a particle is unable to choose its energy state. We are alive because we live. My relationship with Noah is asymptotic* and comes at a price. While this relationship may be symmetrical (beautiful), it is also unstable. Eventually, I too will die and then neither of us will be alive. However, we will have loved and shared together. We will have lived!

Beginning now to understand the point of it all, I am also finally aware of what it is like to share life with an Alaskan Malamute.

---

*Asymptotic as pertaining to a limiting value, for example of a dependent variable, when the independent variable approaches zero or infinity. The "dependent variable" in this case is Noah and I together. The "independent variable" is our finite lifespan as it approaches   zero   (death).

"Inuit whisper the spirits of those who have worn out earthly bone and flesh continue to exist on the other side of the Northern Lights and tell of a legend. There is a place where all Alaskan Malamutes go when they pass from this life to the next..."

The Parameters of Infinity

Technology today makes it possible for companies to genetically replicate animals—cloned images indistinguishable from their original. For anyone willing to spend the money, there are businesses that offer a duplicate of one's canine companion. These cloned images cheapen the original. What makes relationships among living creatures special is that the physical duration is finite. My relationship with Noah is unique because the parameters that allowed us to share it can never be duplicated.

A cloned image looks identical in every respect to the original, but has none of the memories or experiences. The original image can be replicated, but the external variables that shaped it cannot. A "cloned" Noah could never learn what the original knew and recall none of the adventures we shared. "Bunny," "Louis," and "Alien" would just be human sounds, not the names of his favorite chomp toys. He would have no recollection of Shy or Erika. The significance of any relationship is not duration, but quality.

When I was young, I asked my father, "Where do animals go when they die?"

Dad gave it his best and told me that they go to a place called Animal Heaven. That response was good enough as any for a six year-old child. Only when I matured did I begin to comprehend the complexity of what I had asked, realizing an answer is irrelevant unless one fully understands the meaning of the question.

Most modern religions teach only humans possess immortal souls and little regard is given to any other animal. Christianity for example, would have us believe no everlasting relationship with a pet can exist. Humans are supposedly created in the image of a jealous, petty, vindictive god, and if this is the case, I am less than impressed with this alleged Almighty. Take a quick look at the headlines of any day's newspaper. With few exceptions, humans are neither good nor noble creatures. (Maybe they are created in the image of their god after all?) Keeping that in mind, if humans truly do possess souls, I cannot imagine how they can be anything of value. The clergyman cannot prove animals lack eternal spirits any more than he can produce evidence humans possess them.

The pastor is so focused on his perception of "right" that he has become blind to what is true. But then, religion has never been about what is true. It is a controlling and restrictive belief system that embraces superstition and shuns evidence. Akin to an infection, reason is the only cure to this abomination of fear, ignorance, and hate.

The snow and cold have become my final refuge in my total despair. Our time together recedes into the past, yet Noah and I are not getting further apart. Every day that passes is one day closer I am to joining him. Meanwhile, Boreal takes his vengeance, mocking me. A cruel wind now that has neither asked nor given quarter. Standing against the fury, I call out for my Alaskan Malamute—the echo of loneliness reverberating, desperation in the midst of mediocracy that only I am able to hear. Closing my eyes, I can see his face and it becomes clearer as reality fades around me. My affliction is the agony of his loss—a mind now splintered, so utterly broken, that I can no longer discern the difference between it's pieces and the shattered globe that used to contain our world.

While not very spiritual, I have my own idea of what happens when the physical body ceases to function. When an animal lives, wonderful moments are created as they interact with their human companions and, over time, these moments become memories. Though no longer with me, Noah continues to live on through the memories of those lives he touched while here. I am left with something else as well—his love. And, even in the midst of the tumultuous emotions and grief I experience in his absence, I am charged with sharing that. The love he left me is as precious as his life, and I will not waste it.

Have you ever woken in the morning to the sensation of a wet, warm tongue on your hand, yet when you open your eyes there is nothing there? Sometimes in the dark, you might sense something watching you. When the wind blows from the North, can you hear him call? Those having parted with a Malamute can relate to these experiences.

Inuit whisper that the spirits of those who have worn out earthly bone and flesh continue to exist on the other side of the Northern Lights. They tell of a legend: There is a place where all Alaskan Malamutes go when they pass from this life to the next. Beyond the Great Veil that lights the Northern skies, on the Isle of Aurora, gather Tsawake, Windstar, Moonsong, Nanuke and Malko—all the different packs of Alaskan Malamutes. Here, they wait. Proud creatures of the Arctic, all that were sick or old are restored to health and filled with spirit. Those injured or broken are mended and made strong again.

Happy and content, in this land of snow and ice, wind and cold, they run together. A day will come when one stops and looks into the distance. With eyes intent upon what had once been a memory, he lets out a long howl of recognition. Breaking from the pack, he begins to run, powerful legs carrying him faster and faster over the frozen tundra.

When you and your Alaskan Malamute finally meet again, he places his paws upon your shoulders. Reunited at last, "Woo woo," he says. (Translation: "What took you so long?")

While he licks your face, you run your hands through his shimmering coat and once again look into his brown, almond-shaped eyes.

Parting the Great Veil that divides the world of flesh from that of the spirit, you take your first steps into this wondrous new land. Together, you cross over from the finite to the eternal, never to be separated again.

Appendix

The Role of the Alaskan Malamute in the Mahlemut Inuit Culture

Abstract

For thousands of years, the Alaskan Malamute has stood prominently on equal footing with humans. Such a partnership between man and dog was a "vital factor in making life possible in a land generally considered too inhospitable for human beings."[1] Throughout the Kotzebue Sound in Alyeska, the Mahlemut Inuit[2] selectively bred characteristics in their dogs that allowed their culture to not only survive, but flourish in a harsh and bitter land.[3] Strong-willed and fiercely independent, the breed had high expectations of what it demanded from its human companions as well.[4] The Mahlemut Inuit discovered that the interdependence with Alaskan Malamutes permanently changed their culture.[5]

---

[1] Siino, B. (1997). *Alaskan Malamutes: A Complete Pet Owner's Manual.* New York: Barron's.

[2] Beauchamp, R. (1998, December). The Alaskan Malamute: The Golden Rule. *Dog & Kennel, 3,* 6.

[3] Holabach, A. (1998). *A New Owner's Guide to Alaskan Malamutes.* Neptune City: T.F.H. Publications, Inc.

[4] Siino, B. (1995, November). Envy of the Arctic. *Dog Fancy, 26,* 11.

[5] O'Malley, C. (n.d.). *Living with a Malamute...* Retrieved February 10, 2004, from http://www.omalmalamutes.com/

The Role of the Alaskan Malamute
in the Mahlemut Inuit Culture

Introduction

The Mahlemut Inuit culture was significantly impacted by their relationship with their sledge dogs, the Alaskan Malamute. A partnership that spanned thousands of years, these dogs stood prominently on equal footing with their human companions—working, hunting, and living alongside them. The interdependent relationship between Mahlemut Inuit and Alaskan Malamute fostered prosperity among both and enabled them not just to survive, but to flourish in the inhospitable land above the Arctic Circle.

Review of the Literature

There is a significant amount of literature that exists, both online and in print, detailing the impact of the Alaskan Malamute on the Mahlemut Inuit culture. Sources cover both the history and unique needs of the Mahlemut Inuit and their dogs, the breed known today as the Alaskan Malamute. Much is also written about how well the Alaskan Malamute was suited to meet those unique needs of the Mahlemut Inuit and what characteristics allow them even today to thrive in a cold, inhospitable land.

Having migrated from Asia, the Inuit of Canada (2003) states that, for thousands of years Inuit tribes of the Inuvialuit populated the region known to us today as Alaska. Anthropologists believe the dog was domesticated about six thousand years ago and the so-called Spitz, or Arctic type of dog migrated with them (Riddle & Seeley, 1988). Each tribe developed characteristics in their dogs that they felt would be beneficial. Crossing the Bering Strait approximately four thousand years ago, one such tribe, known as the Mahlemut, settled the area in and around Kotzebue Sound. Thousands of years later, between 1740 and 1890, Westerners discovered the Inuit people living prosperously in that brutal Arctic land. The Mahlemut were notable for their exceptionally beautiful and tirelessly working dogs. It did not escape the attention of these early Arctic explorers that these dogs were as strong-minded and strong-willed as their owners.

The Alaskan Malamute is a multifaceted dog that was bred for its intelligence, maneuverability, and strength. Easily able to tolerate the extreme cold of the Arctic, Malamutes possess great stamina and are willing to work under killing conditions on near starvation diets. The Mahlemut Inuit treasured their dogs and treated them as family members (Adamson, 2002). The fondness Alaskan Malamutes expressed for the Inuit is evident even today in the way they continue to bond with their contemporary human companions.

In addition to their intelligence, maneuverability, stamina, strength, and disposition, the Alaskan Malamute's physical attributes are detailed in the

American Kennel Club's Breed Standard. Examination of these characteristics—traits the Inuit specifically bred for—reveal exactly how and why the dog performs so well in brutal Arctic conditions. The American Kennel Club's (2004) Breed Standard for the Alaskan Malamute states that, "The Malamute must be a heavy boned dog with sound legs, good feet, deep chest and powerful shoulders, and have all of the other physical attributes necessary for the efficient performance of his job. The gait must be steady, balanced, tireless and totally efficient. The Malamute is structured for strength and endurance, and any characteristic of the individual specimen, including temperament, which interferes with the accomplishment of this purpose, is to be considered the most serious of faults." Alaskan Malamutes are dual-coated, possessing both a coarse guard coat and a woolly undercoat. The guard coat sheds snow and protects them from wind while the undercoat insulates them against subzero temperatures. The abundance of fur around the neck and chest area further protects their vital organs. Holaback (1998, p. 9) notes that "their small prick ears are not easily frostbitten and the muzzle has sufficient length to warm frigid air before it reaches the lungs. Leg length is sufficient to keep the chest and abdomen above the snow line." Tails are carried up over the back like a plume rather than trailing behind in the snow. When forced to sleep out of cover, the Malamute curls up and the tail is long enough to wrap over the nose, preventing frostbite.

The Alaskan Malamute's versatility served the Mahlemut Inuit in many ways, and without the help of their dogs, it is possible their culture would have perished on the ice at some point in history. Three areas the Mahlemut required help in were transportation, hunting, and herding. Specifically, they needed assistance in pulling sledges over long distances and in tracking (seals) and herding (polar bears) their game (Alaskan Malamute Club of America, 2002).

The Alaskan Malamute had needs of its own necessary for its survival in the Arctic and held high expectations of what it demanded from its human partners. It was expected of the Mahlemut Inuit to provide food, companionship, and guidance. Malamutes required a high-quality meat-based diet (Siino, 1995), and while "their efficient metabolisms required less fuel than one would expect from so large an animal" (Siino, 1997, p. 6), they would not have been useful in helping meet the needs of others if they were off searching for food to satisfy needs of their own. It is important to note that the Alaskan Malamute lived and worked *with* their human companions, *not* for them. They demanded that their "instincts, body language, and vocalizations be respected, and when appropriate, heeded. To do otherwise could mean death to both the people and the dogs, when, say, the musher guiding the sled failed to heed the lead dog's warning of a crevasse in the ice" (Siino, 1997, p. 13). Already noted as being strong-willed and fiercely independent, Malamutes are also pack-oriented and sensitive to the pack order. The Mahlemut did not command as a master, but rather as an "alpha."

The Mahlemut Inuit were both firm and compassionate with their dogs, treating them much better than other Inuit tribes (Woolf, 2004). While aware of the sturdy constitution and the Alaskan Malamute's high tolerance for pain and discomfort, they also understood that "a Malamute is completely incapable of withstanding being struck in anger (Holaback, 1998). Woolf (2004) notes that Linda Smith, a Malamute owner and rescue coordinator in Mount Gilead, Ohio, stressed the breed's intelligence and strong will as major traits and emphasized the need for firm obedience training using positive reinforcement rather than punishment. "Malamutes need gentle, firm training," she said. "No pinch collars, no hanging, no beating, no choking the dog until it turns blue. Positive reinforcement is so much better."

Theoretical Applications

Functionalist Perspective. Defined by Henslin (2003), functional analysis is a "theoretical framework in which society is viewed as composed of various parts, each with a function that, when fulfilled, contributes to society's equilibrium." Undoubtedly, the Alaskan Malamute was integral to the Mahlemut Inuit's existence in Kotzebue Sound, Alaska. To understand Mahlemut culture, one must realize that it was structured for survival in the Arctic. The Alaskan Malamute fulfilled numerous functions that not only allowed the Mahlemut people to survive, but to prosper in that harsh inhospitable land. Food and transportation were essential. The Mahlemut dogs tracked game; hunted seals and herded polar bears. Additionally, the Malamutes were able to transport both kill and supplies back to the village. While the Inuit might be able to haul small loads on sleds over short distances, the strength and stamina of the Malamute was essential to freight the larger sledges over the barren expanses between village and food source.

Conflict Perspective. Conflict theory is a "theoretical framework in which society is viewed as composed of groups competing for scarce resources" (Henslin, 2003). Resources above the Arctic Circle are limited and thus there is fierce competition for food. Additionally, the harsh environment fosters both independence of thought and a competitive pack order necessary for survival. While on the surface Mahlemut Inuit and their dogs appear congenial (and it certainly is mutually beneficial to both), there is a definite struggle for power that permeates the relationship. The dominating nature of the Alaskan Malamute resists the Mahlemut Inuit's attempts on them of conformity. Submission was forced through physical means (such as harnesses), punishment, and the reward of food. Additionally, Alaskan Malamutes were selectively bred for temperament. Those dogs with a poor disposition were not bred and often time were killed.

Symbolic Interaction Perspective. Henslin (2003) defines symbolic interactionism as "a theoretical perspective in which society is viewed as composed of symbols that people use to establish meaning, develop their views of the world, and communicate with one another." The Alaskan Malamute among the Mahlemut Inuit was a symbol of success and prosperity, emblematizing freedom and abundance. Freedom to transport heavy loads over long distances and abundance of meat and furs through successful hunting. The roles of both man and dog in the Mahlemut Inuit culture were clearly defined: The Mahlemuts provided food, water, shelter, a prominent place in the family, discipline, and a purpose. In return, they could expect the Alaskan Malamutes to pull their sledges, hunt, and herd.

Conclusion

While both functionalist and conflict perspectives adequately examine this interdependent relationship, it is the perspective of symbolic interaction that is remarkably effective in analyzing the profound impact of the Alaskan Malamute on the Mahlemut Inuit culture. The roles of both man and dog are clearly defined and easily understood. The inherent symbolism of the Alaskan Malamute—the freedom and abundance it conferred to its human companions in a harsh and bitter Arctic land—convincingly illustrates how it was an integral part of and permanently changed the Mahlemut Inuit culture.

References

Adamson, E. (2002, April). Pulling Their Weight. *Dog Fancy 33,* 4.

Alaskan Malamute Club of America. (2008). *The Alaskan Malamute – An Introduction.* Retrieved August 11, 2011, from, http://www.alaskanmalamute.org/

American Kennel Club. (2011). *The Alaskan Malamute: Breed Standard.* Retrieved August 11, 2011, from http://www.akc.org/breeds/alaskan_malamute/

Henslin, J. M. (2003). *Sociology: A Down-To-Earth Approach (6th ed.)*. Boston: Allyn and Bacon.

Holabach, A. (1998). *A New Owner's Guide to Alaskan Malamutes*. Neptune City: T.F.H. Publications, Inc.

Inuit of Canada. (2003). *Inuit Kanatami*. Ottawa: Inuit Tapiriit Kanatami.

Riddle, M., & Seeley, E. (1988). *The Complete Alaskan Malamute*. New York: Howell Book House.

Siino, B. (1997). *Alaskan Malamutes: A Complete Pet Owner's Manual*. New York: Barron's.

Siino, B. (1995, November). Envy of the Arctic. *Dog Fancy, 26,* 11.

Woolf, N. B. (2011). *Dog Owner's Guide: The Alaskan Malamute*. Retrieved August 11, 2011, from http://www.canismajor.com/dog/malamute.html